VOL. 44

HAL•LEONARD

GUITAR PLAY·ALONG®

JAZZ Greats

T0055383

ISBN-13: 978-0-634-09444-6
ISBN-10: 0-634-09444-0

Visit Hal Leonard Online at www.halleonard.com

HAL•LEONARD®
CORPORATION
7777 W. BLUEMOUND RD. P.O. BOX 13819
MILWAUKEE, WISCONSIN 53213

Guitar Notation Legend

THE MUSICAL STAFF shows pitches and rhythms and is divided by bar lines into measures. Pitches are named after the first seven letters of the alphabet.

TABLATURE graphically represents the guitar fingerboard. Each horizontal line represents a string, and each number represents a fret.

Notes:

Strings:

4th string, 2nd fret   1st & 2nd strings open, played together   open D chord

HALF-STEP BEND: Strike the note and bend up 1/2 step.

WHOLE-STEP BEND: Strike the note and bend up one step.

GRACE NOTE BEND: Strike the note and bend up as indicated. The first note does not take up any time.

SLIGHT (MICROTONE) BEND: Strike the note and bend up 1/4 step.

BEND AND RELEASE: Strike the note and bend up as indicated, then release back to the original note. Only the first note is struck.

PRE-BEND: Bend the note as indicated, then strike it.

VIBRATO: The string is vibrated by rapidly bending and releasing the note with the fretting hand.

PALM MUTING: The note is partially muted by the pick hand lightly touching the string(s) just before the bridge.

HAMMER-ON: Strike the first (lower) note with one finger, then sound the higher note (on the same string) with another finger by fretting it without picking.

PULL-OFF: Place both fingers on the notes to be sounded. Strike the first note and without picking, pull the finger off to sound the second (lower) note.

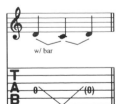

LEGATO SLIDE: Strike the first note and then slide the same fret-hand finger up or down to the second note. The second note is not struck.

SHIFT SLIDE: Same as legato slide, except the second note is struck.

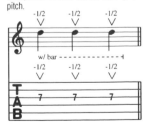

TRILL: Very rapidly alternate between the notes indicated by continuously hammering on and pulling off.

TAPPING: Hammer ("tap") the fret indicated with the pick-hand index or middle finger and pull off to the note fretted by the fret hand.

NATURAL HARMONIC: Strike the note while the fret-hand lightly touches the string directly over the fret indicated.

PINCH HARMONIC: The note is fretted normally and a harmonic is produced by adding the edge of the thumb or the tip of the index finger of the pick hand to the normal pick attack.

TREMOLO PICKING: The note is picked as rapidly and continuously as possible.

VIBRATO BAR DIVE AND RETURN: The pitch of the note or chord is dropped a specified number of steps (in rhythm) then returned to the original pitch.

VIBRATO BAR SCOOP: Depress the bar just before striking the note, then quickly release the bar.

VIBRATO BAR DIP: Strike the note and then immediately drop a specified number of steps, then release back to the original pitch.

Additional Musical Definitions

(accent)	• Accentuate note (play it louder)	

(staccato)	• Play the note short

D.S. al Coda — • Go back to the sign (𝄋), then play until the measure marked **"To Coda,"** then skip to the section labelled **"Coda."**

D.C. al Fine — • Go back to the beginning of the song and play until the measure marked **"Fine"** (end).

Fill — • Label used to identify a brief melodic figure which is to be inserted into the arrangement.

N.C. — • No Chord

• Repeat measures between signs.

1. **2.** — • When a repeated section has different endings, play the first ending only the first time and the second ending only the second time.

CONTENTS

Page	Title	Demo Track	Play-Along Track
4	I Remember You TAL FARLOW	1	2
30	I'll Remember April GRANT GREEN	3	4
50	Impressions PAT MARTINO	5	6
15	In a Mellow Tone JOE PASS	7	8
62	Moonlight in Vermont JOHNNY SMITH	9	10
66	On a Slow Boat to China BARNEY KESSEL	11	12
73	Things Ain't the Way They Used to Be JIM HALL	13	14
80	Yesterdays WES MONTGOMERY	15	16
	TUNING NOTES	17	

I Remember You

from the Paramount Picture THE FLEET'S IN
Words by Johnny Mercer
Music by Victor Schertzinger

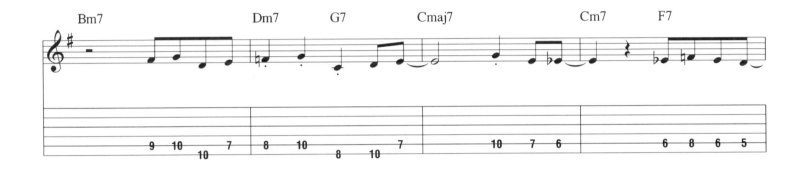

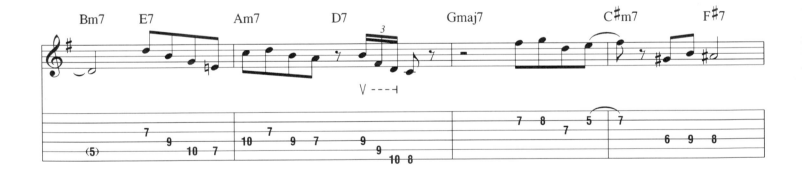

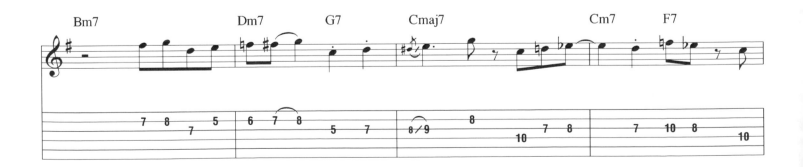

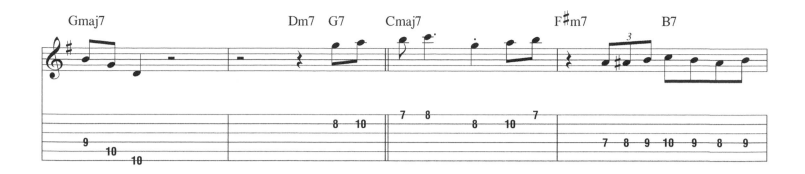

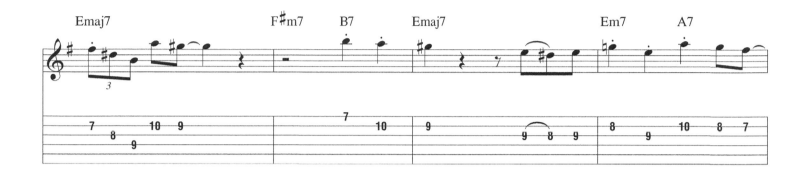

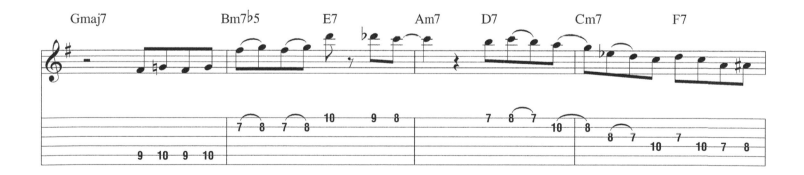

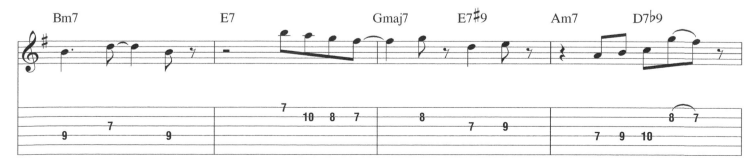

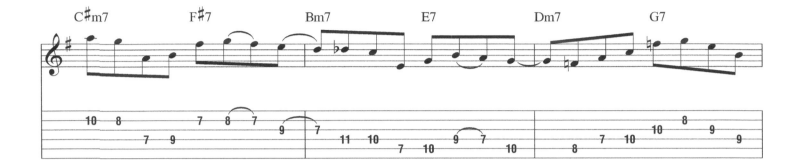

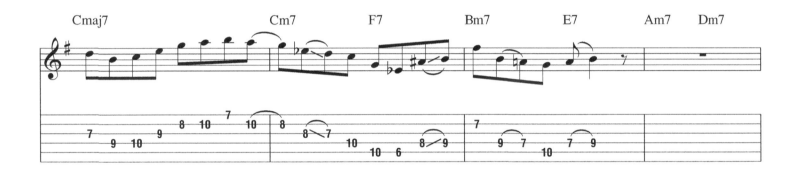

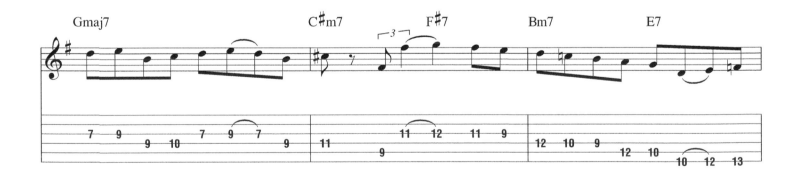

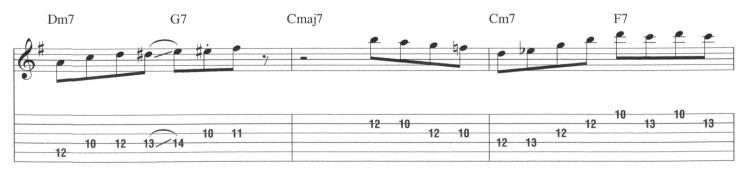

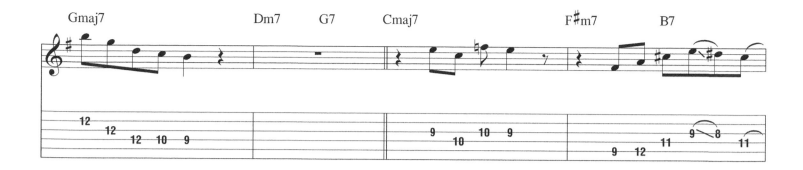

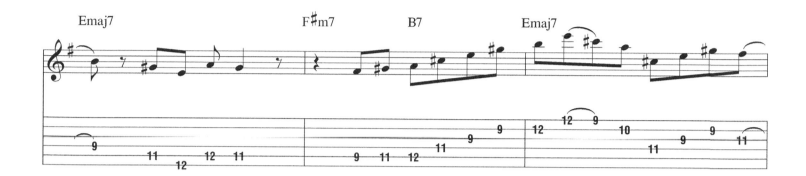

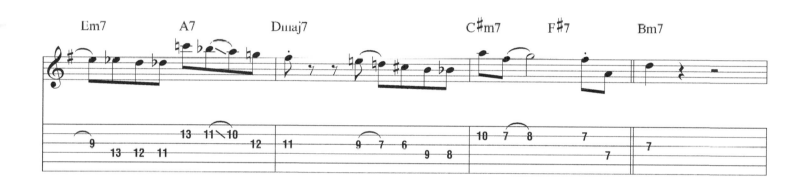

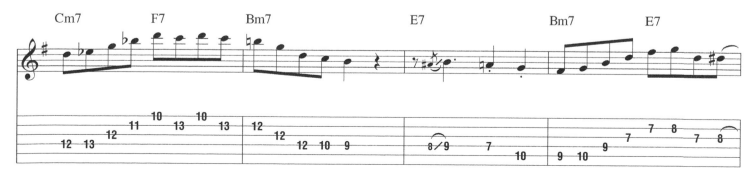

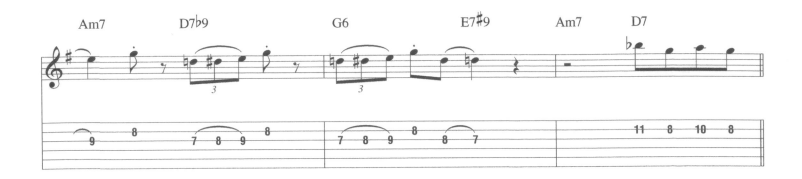

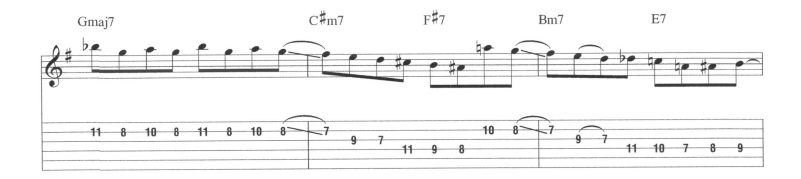

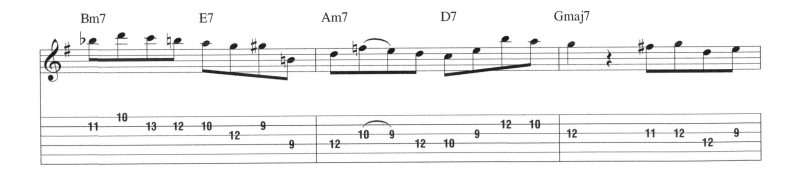

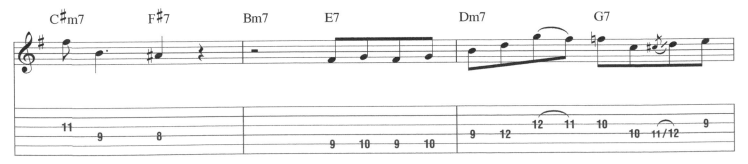

8

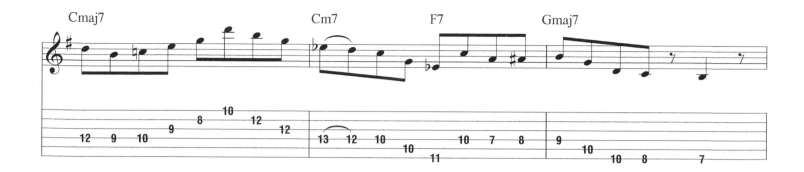

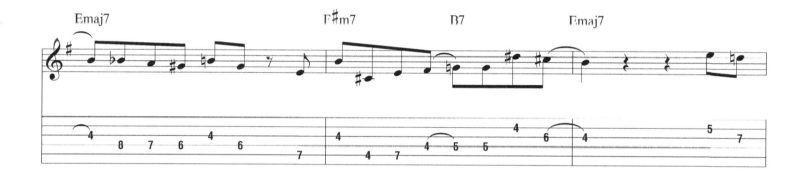

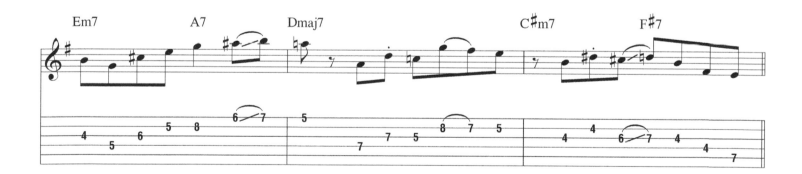

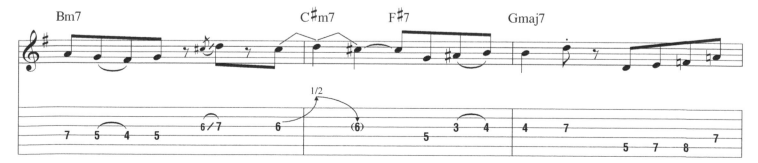

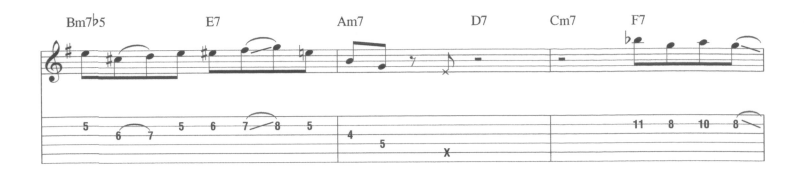

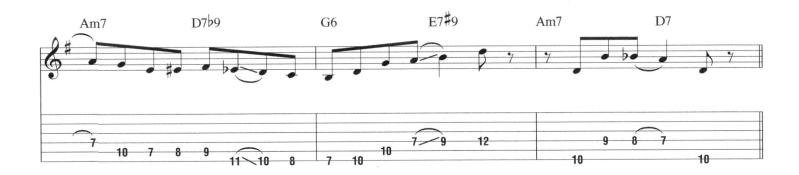

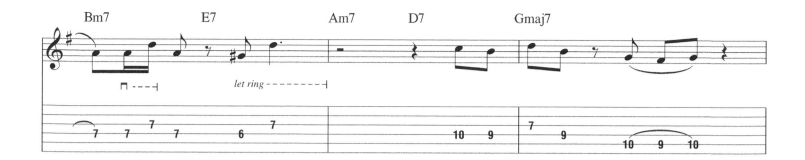

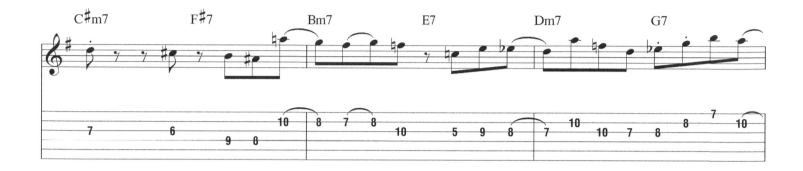

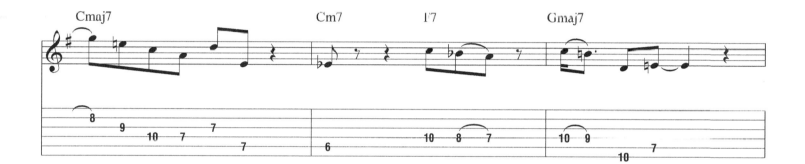

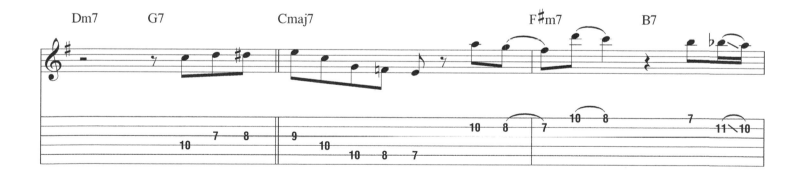

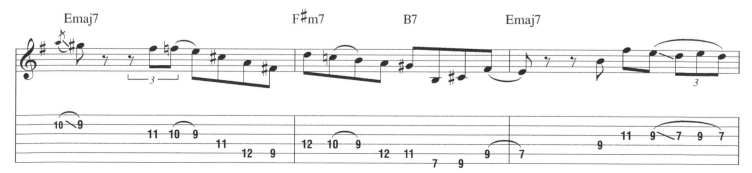

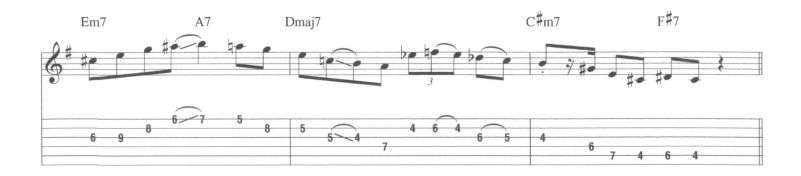

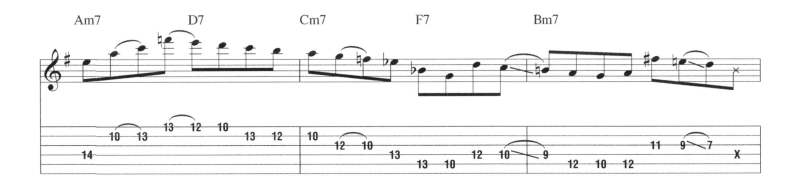

D Piano Solo

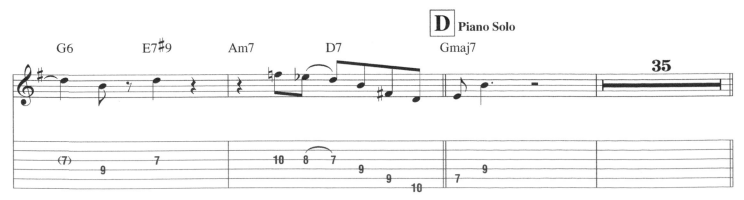

12

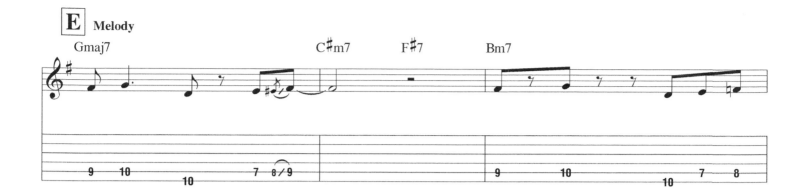

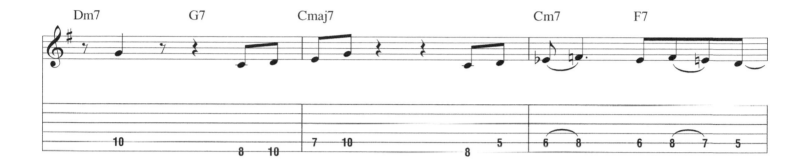

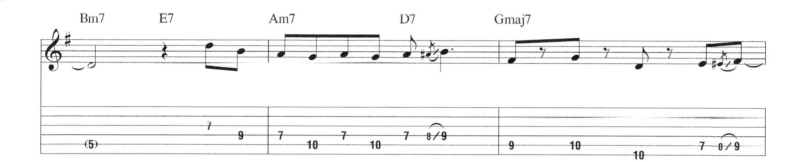

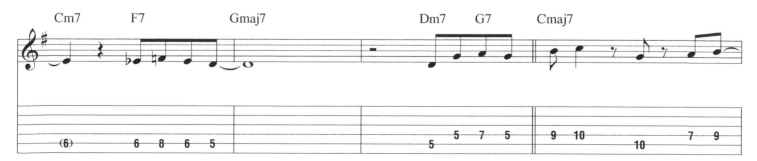

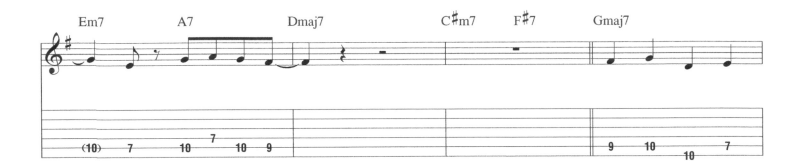

14

In a Mellow Tone

By Duke Ellington

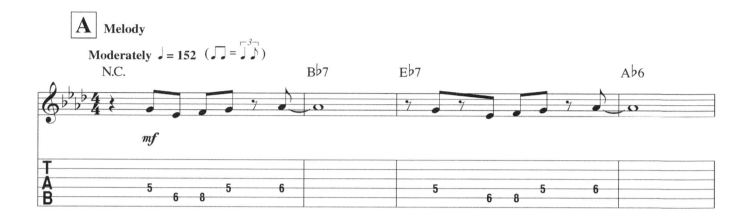

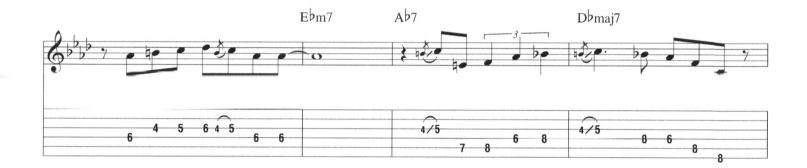

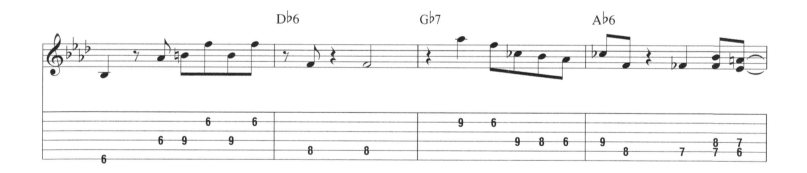

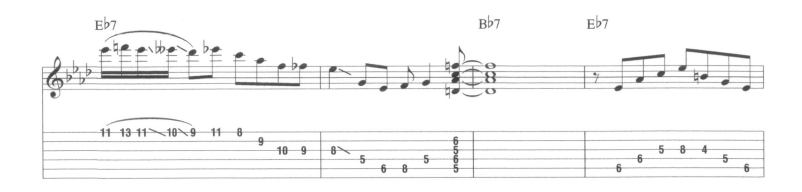

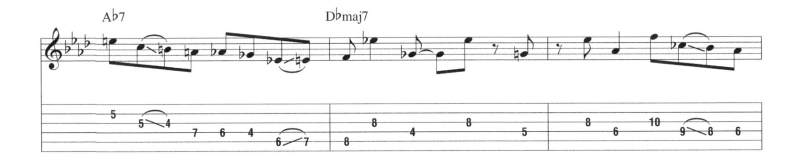

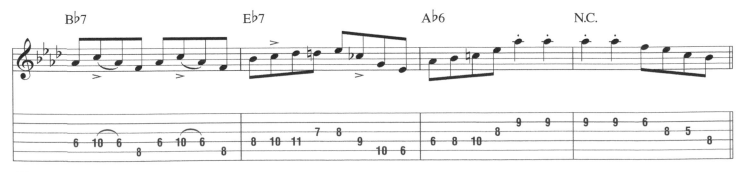

B Guitar Solo

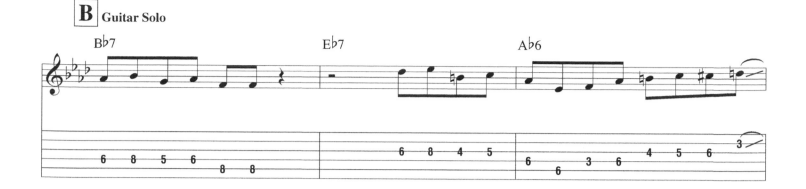

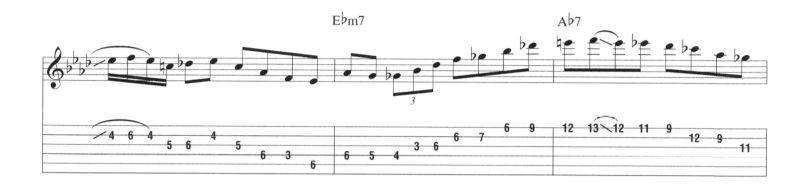

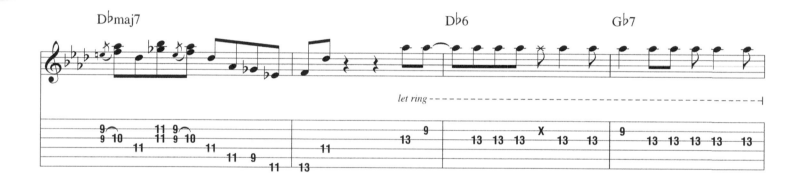

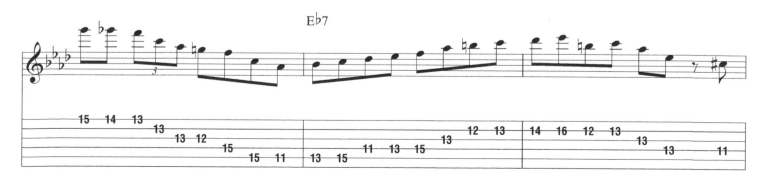

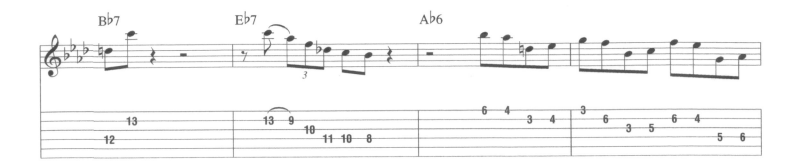

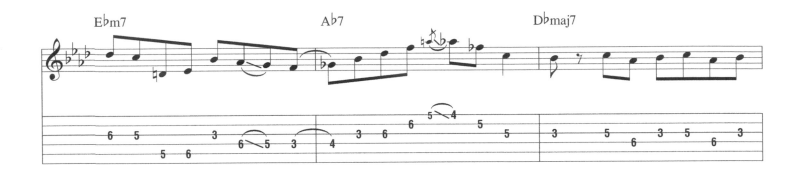

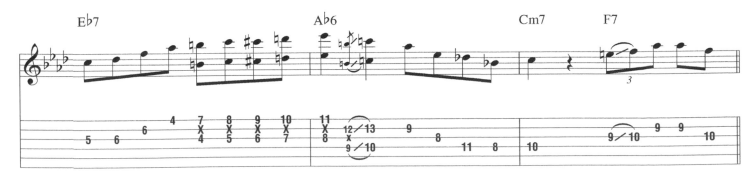

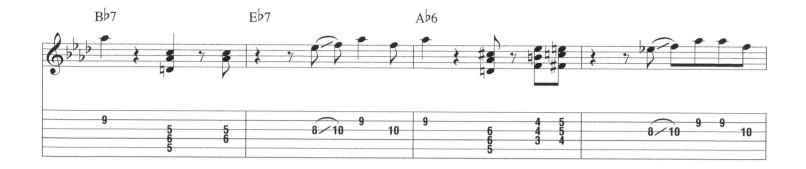

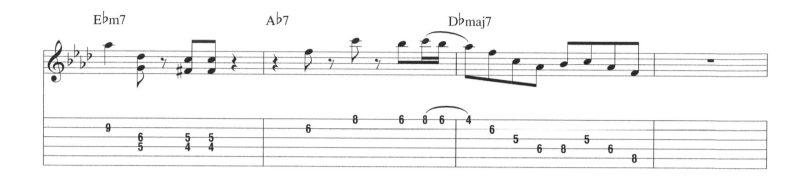

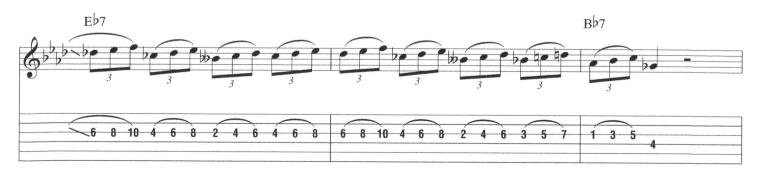

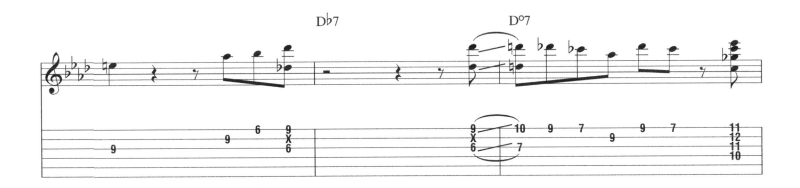

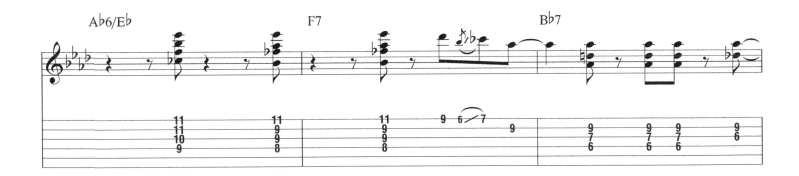

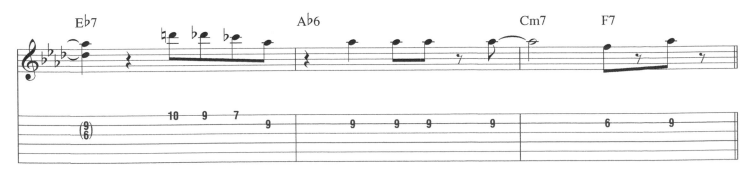

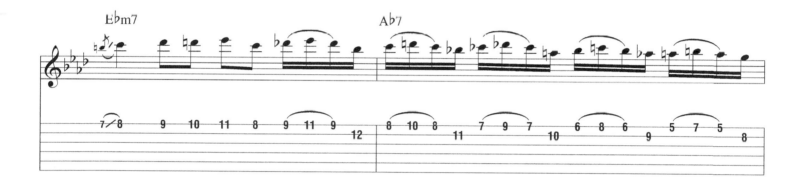

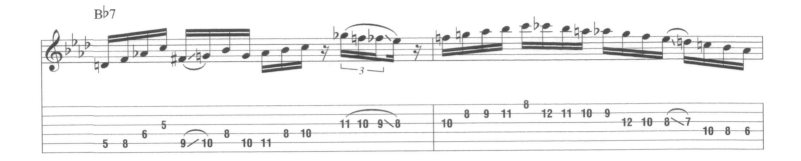

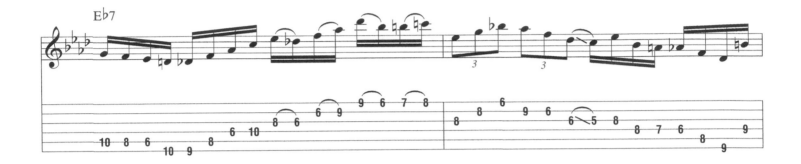

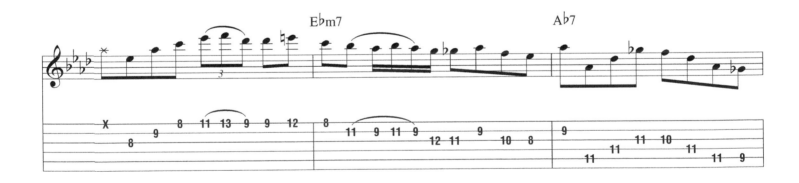

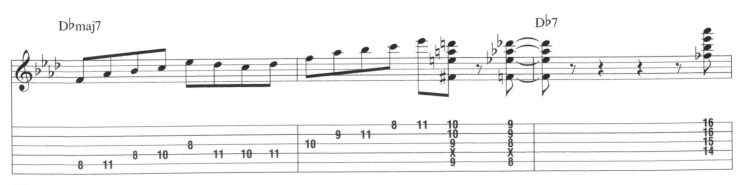

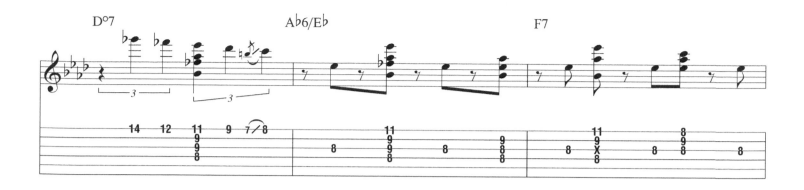

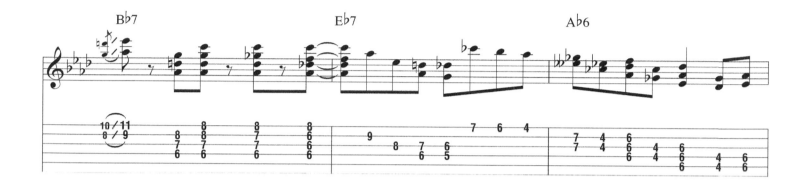

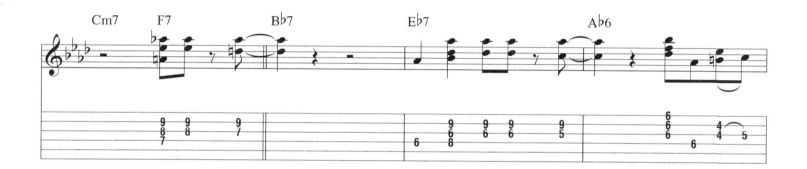

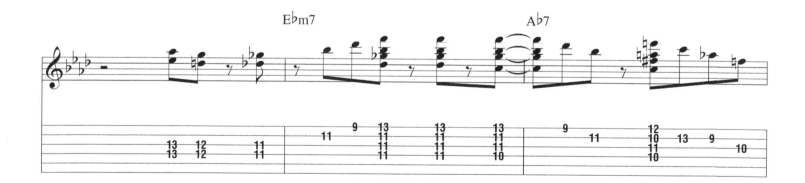

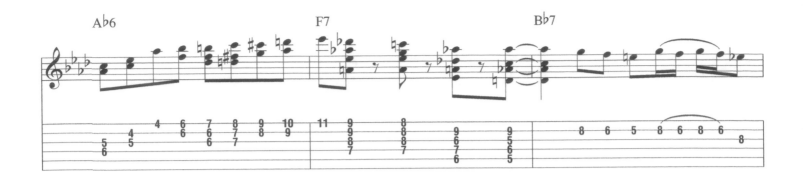

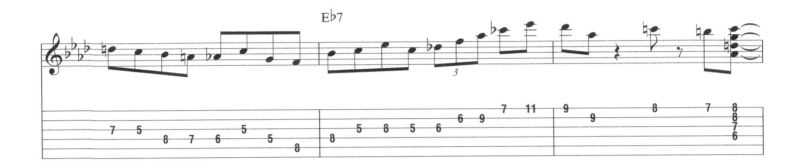

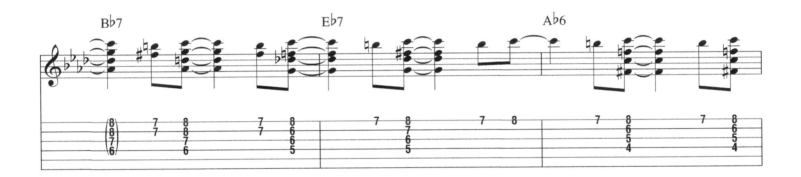

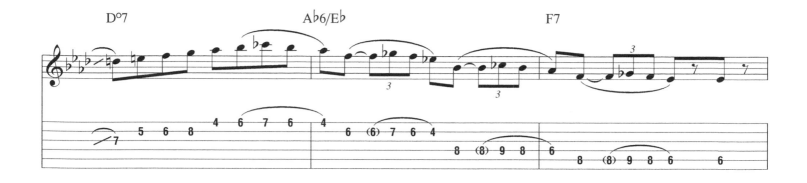

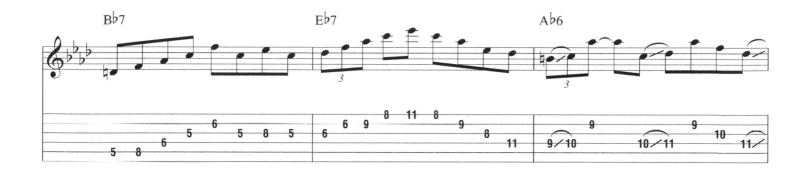

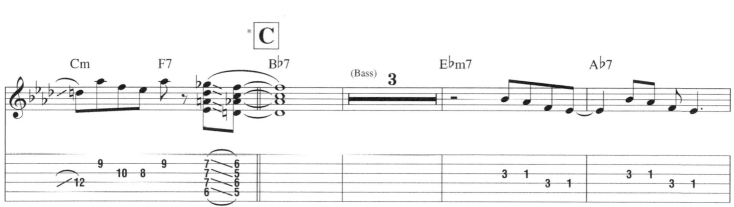

*Gtr. and bass exchange 4 meas. solos ("trade fours") throughout section.

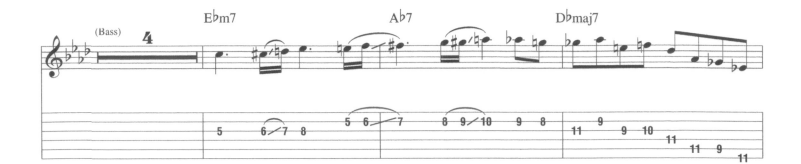

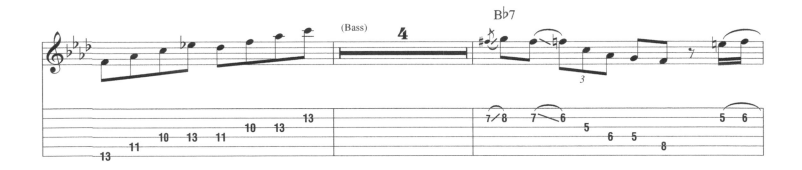

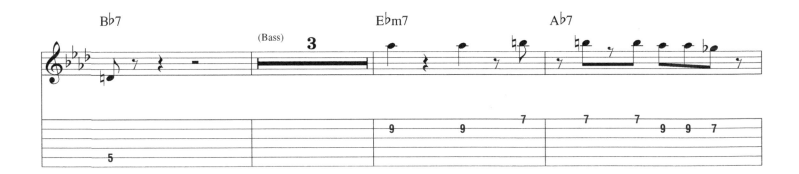

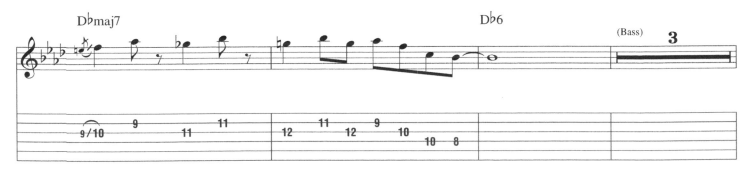

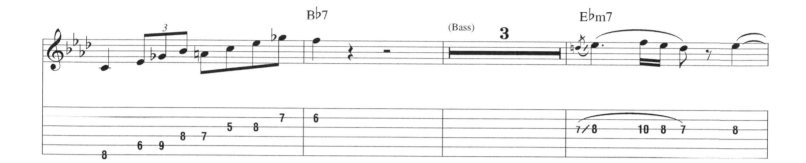

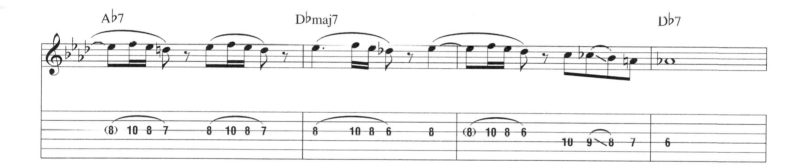

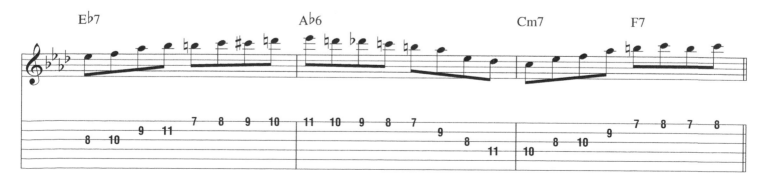

D Guitar Solo

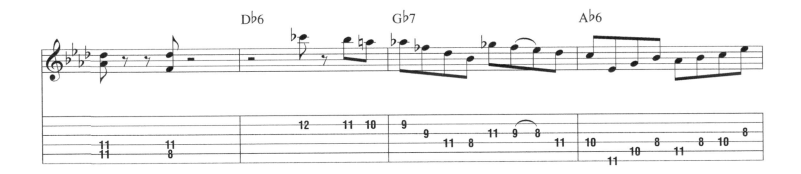

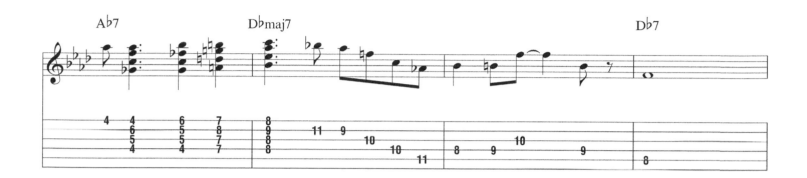

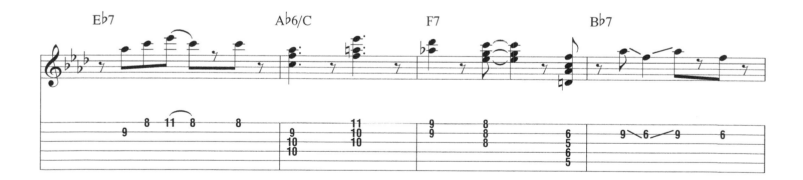

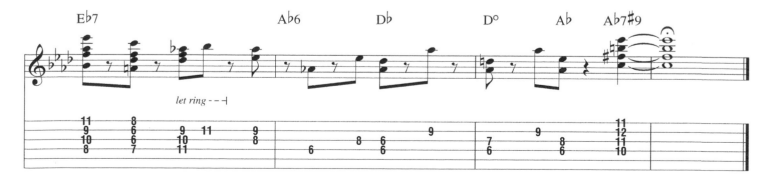

I'll Remember April

Words and Music by Pat Johnston, Don Raye and Gene De Paul

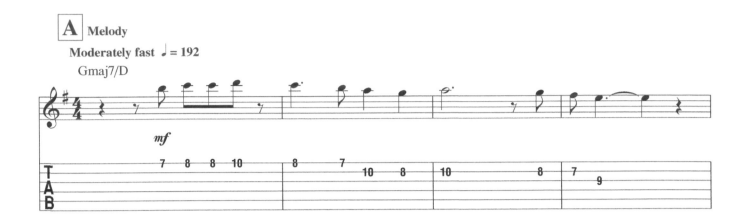

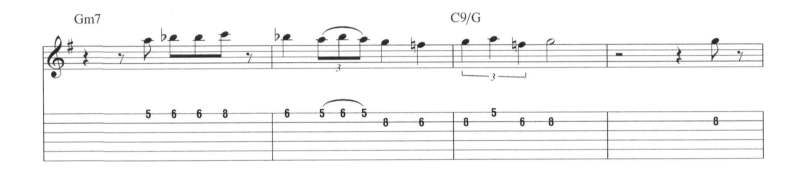

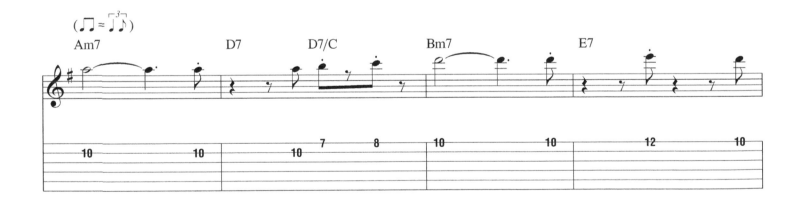

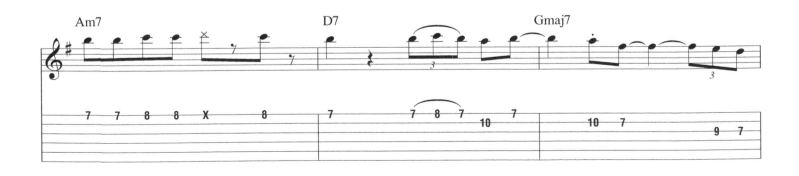

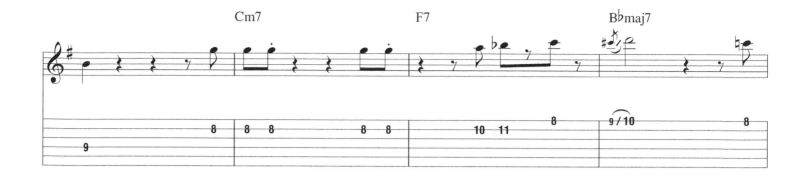

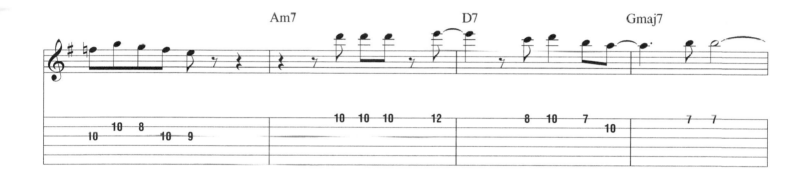

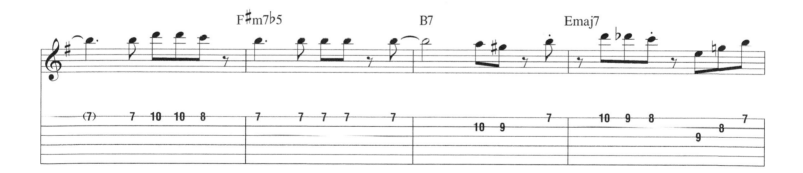

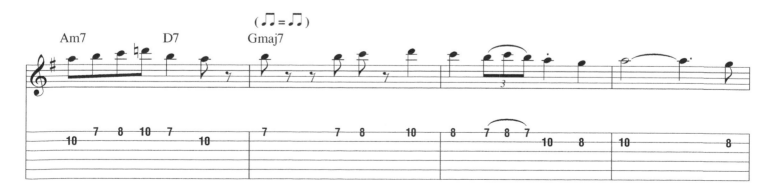

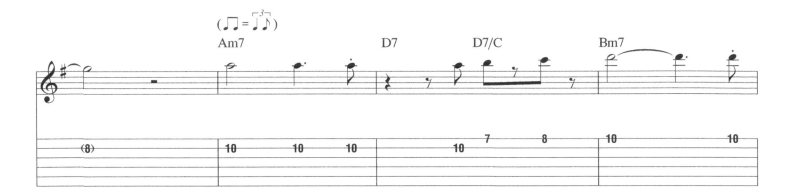

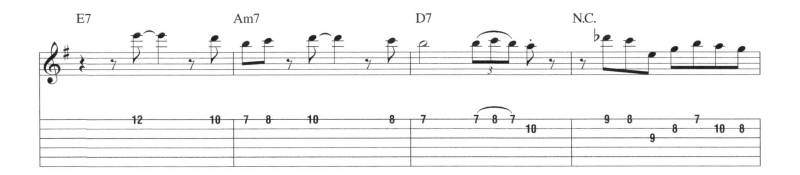

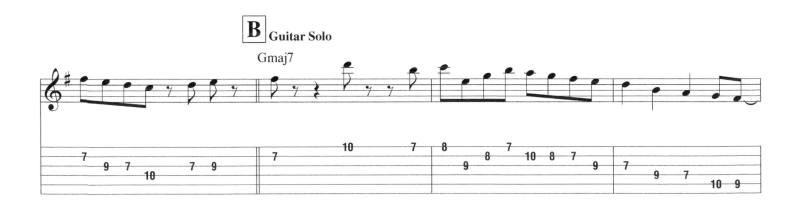

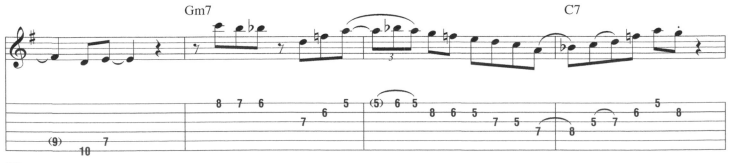

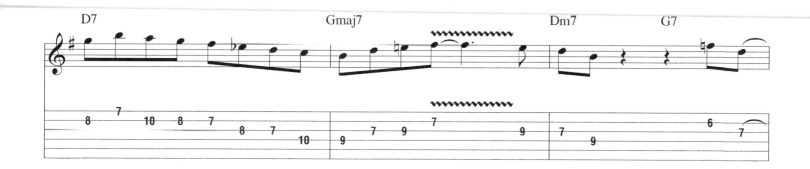

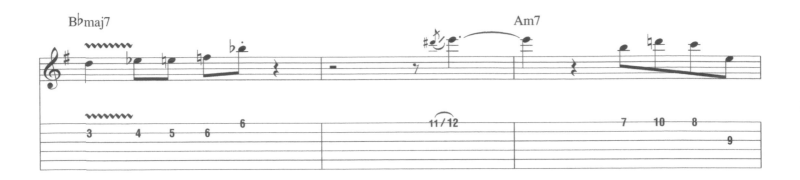

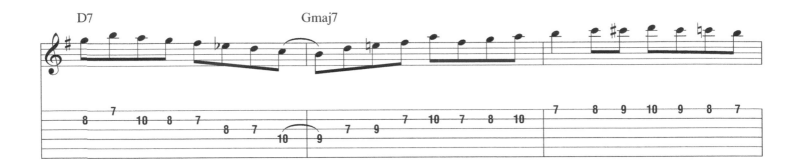

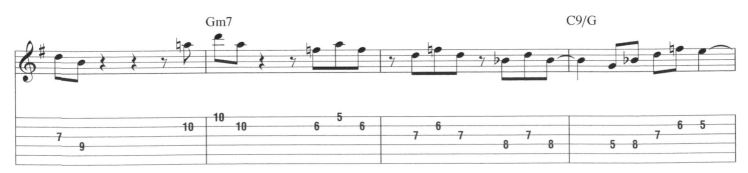

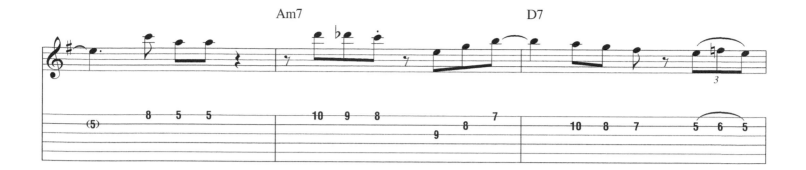

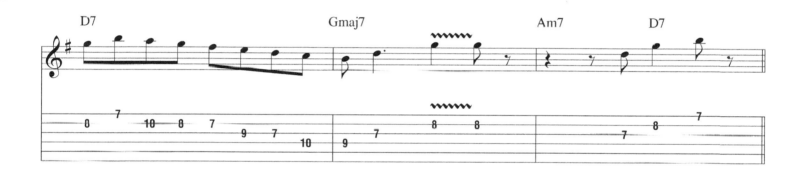

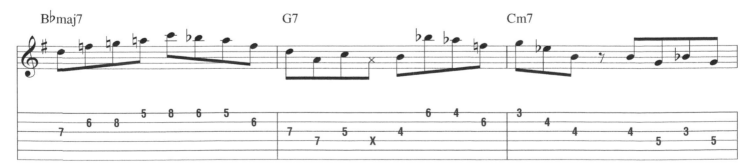

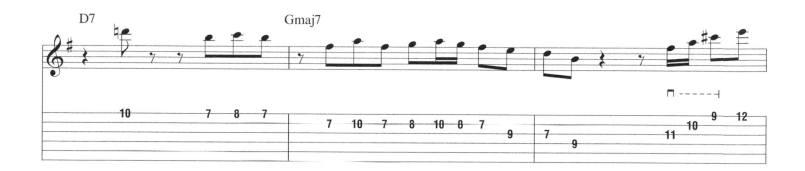

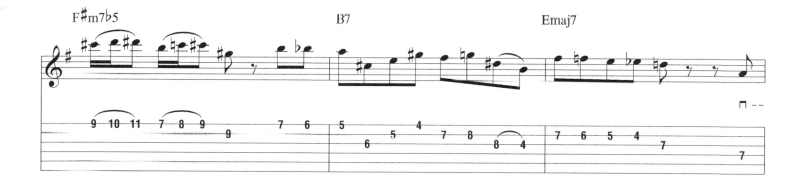

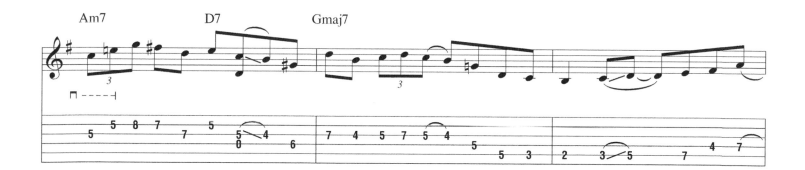

C9

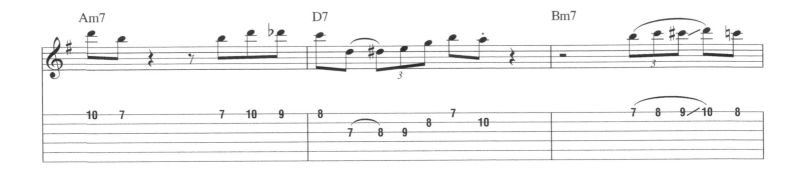

Am7   D7   Bm7

E7   Am7   D7

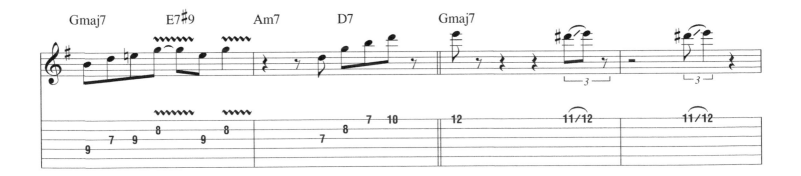

Gmaj7   E7#9   Am7   D7   Gmaj7

Gm7

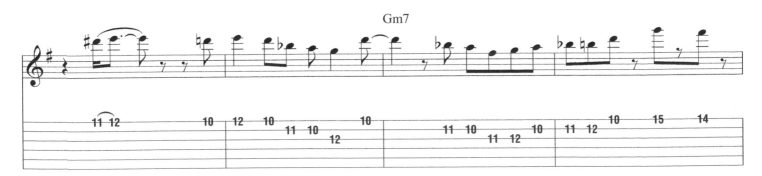

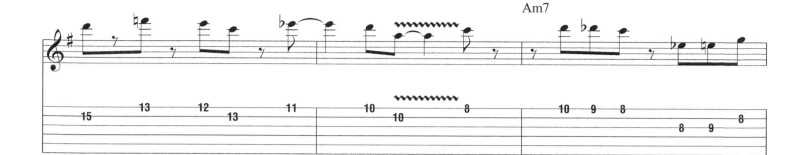

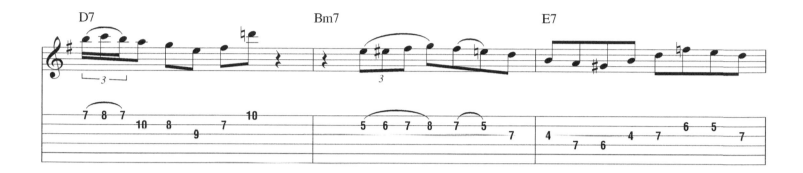

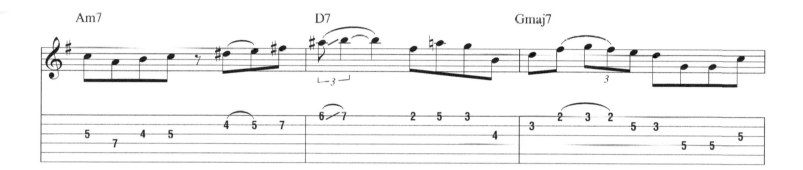

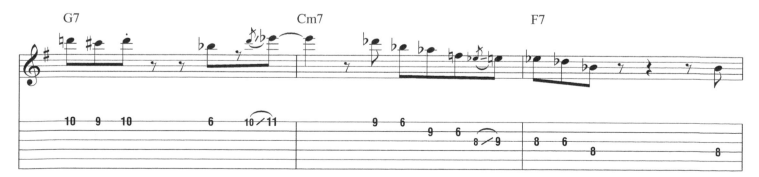

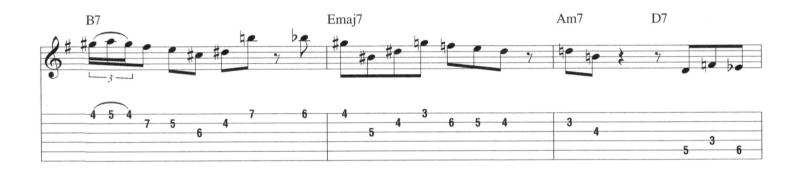

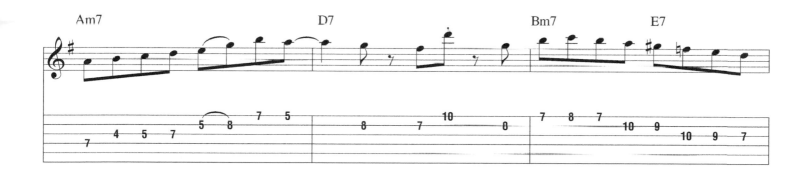

*\boxed{C}

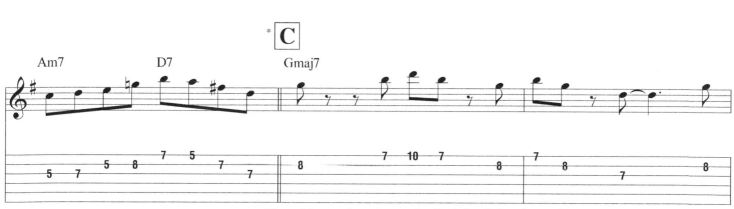

*Gtr. and drums exchange 4 meas. solos ("trade fours") throughout section.

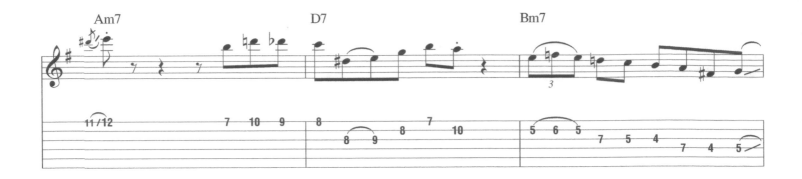

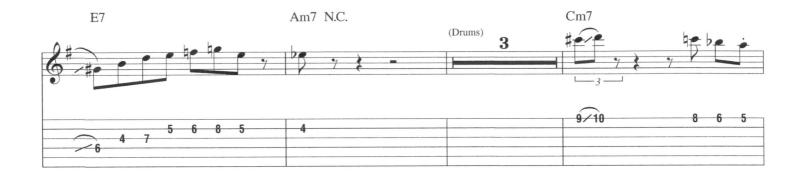

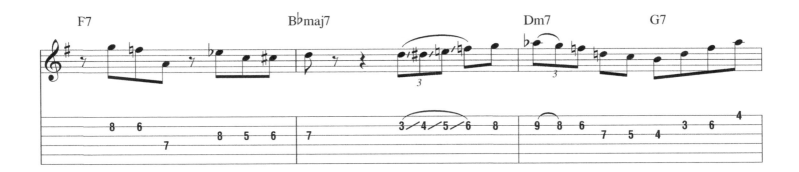

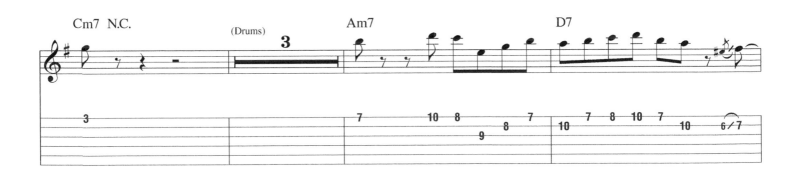

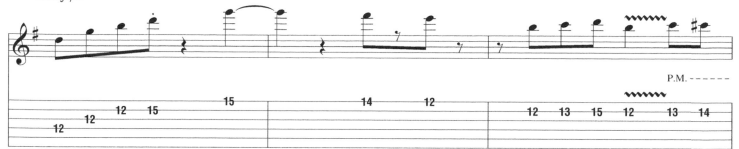

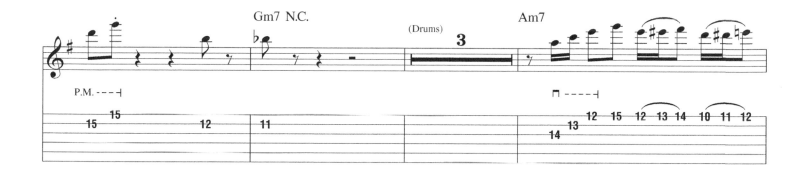

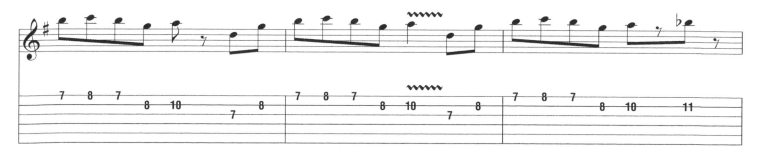

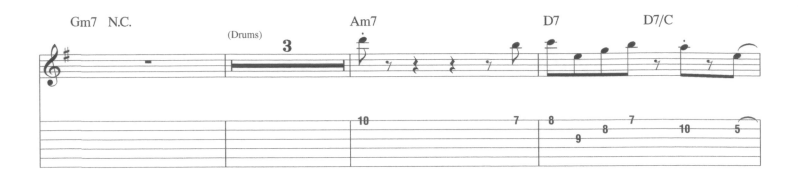

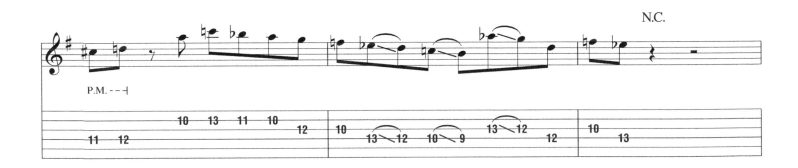

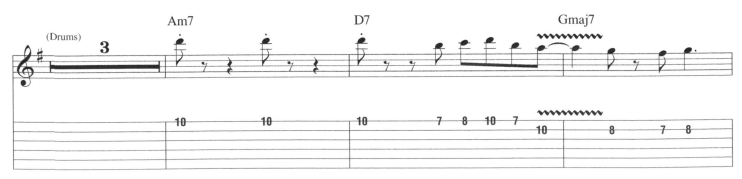

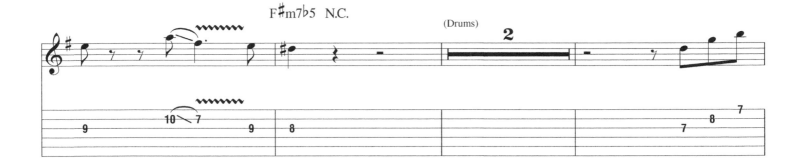

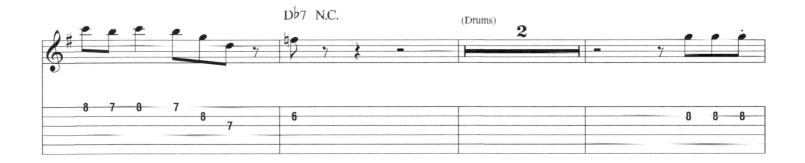

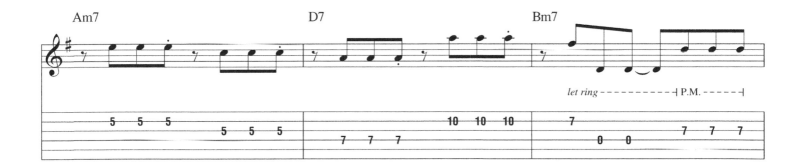

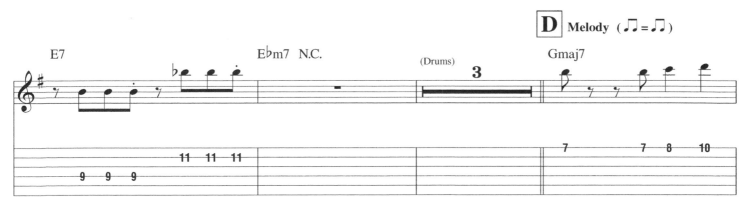

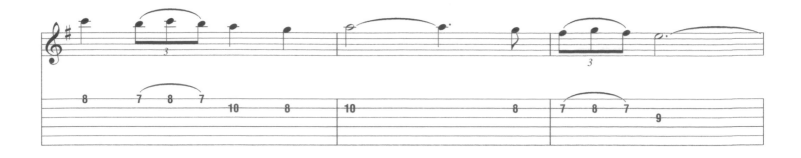

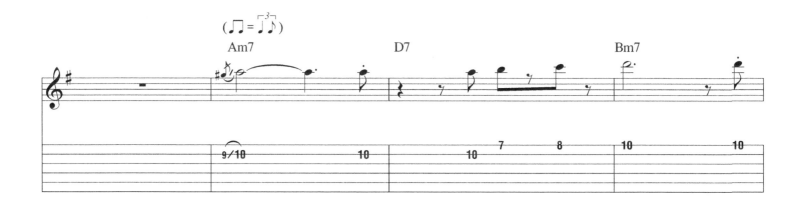

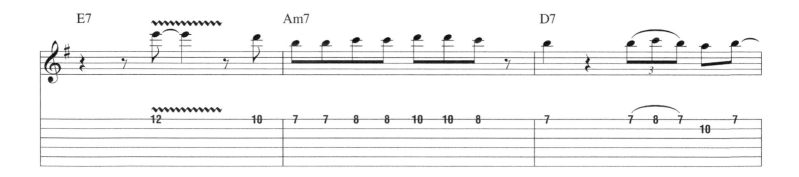

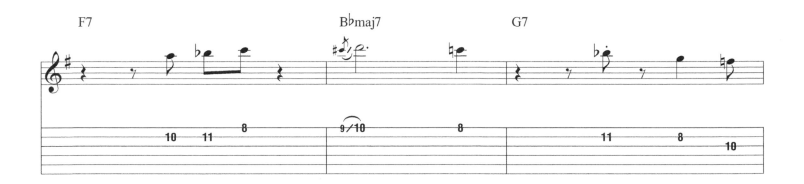

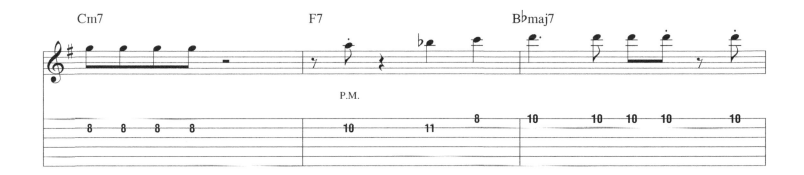

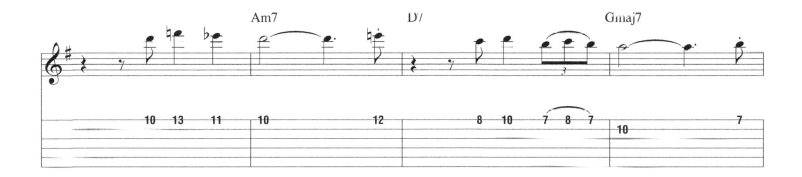

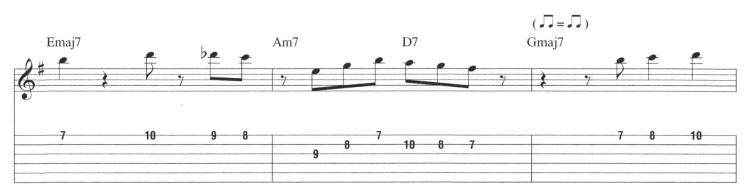

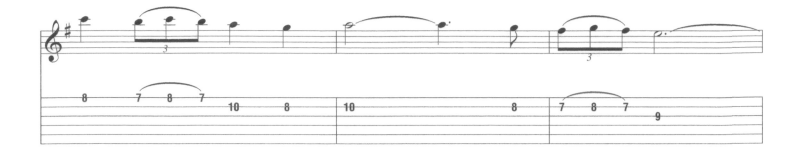

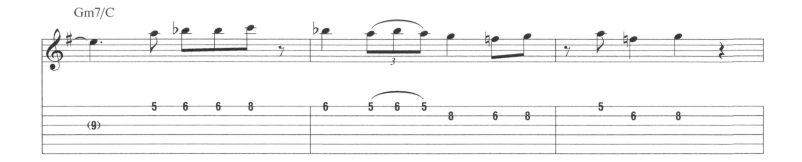

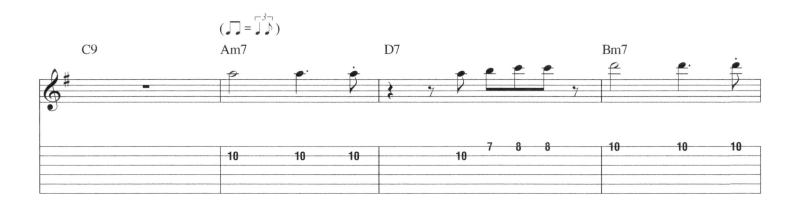

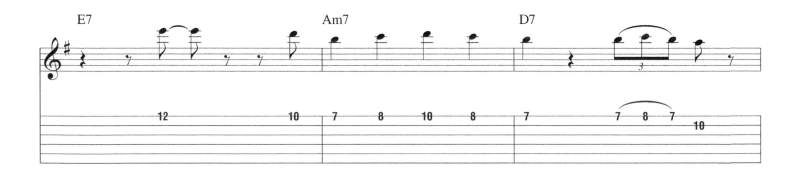

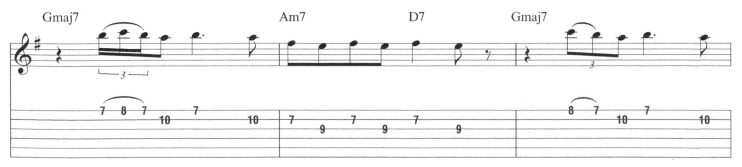

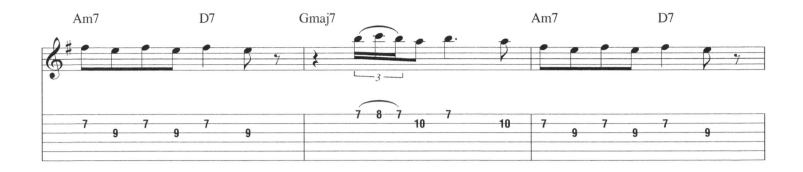

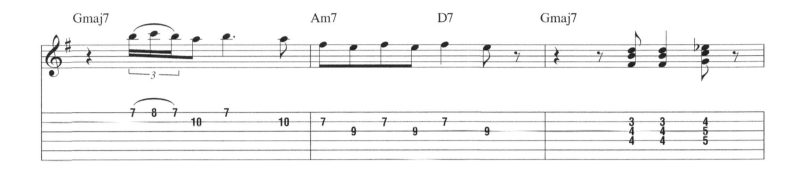

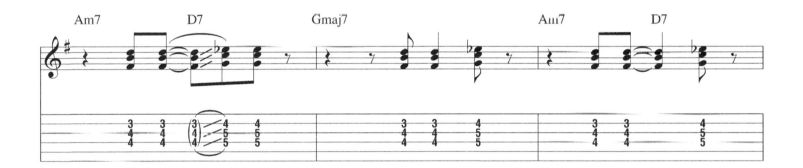

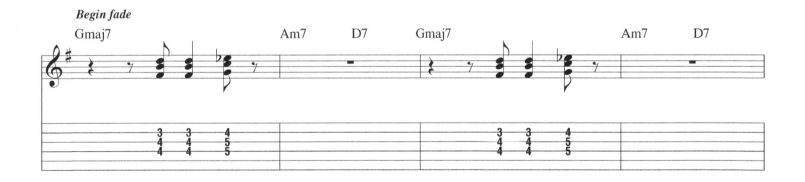

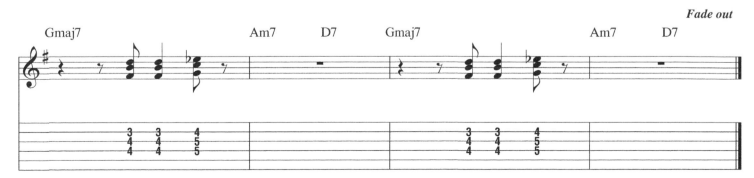

Impressions

By John Coltrane

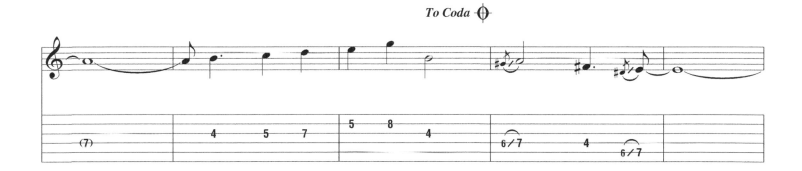

Bbm7

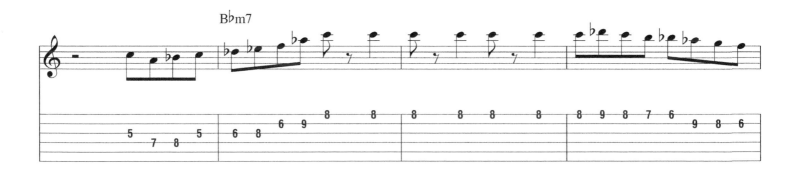

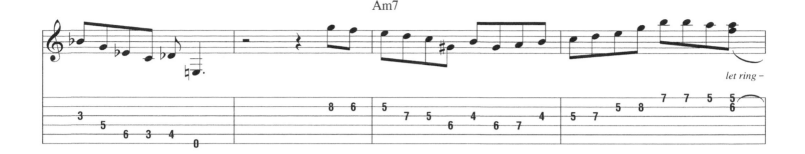

B♭m7

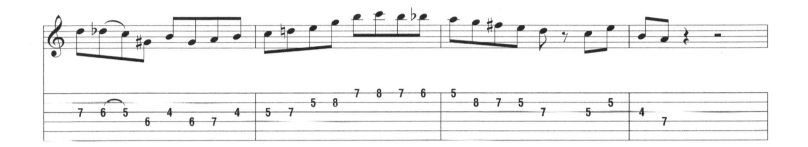

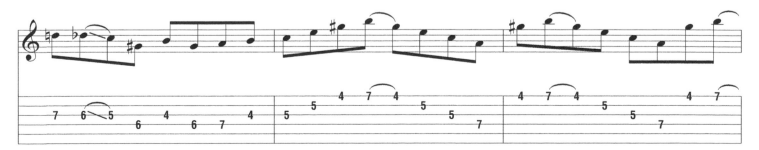

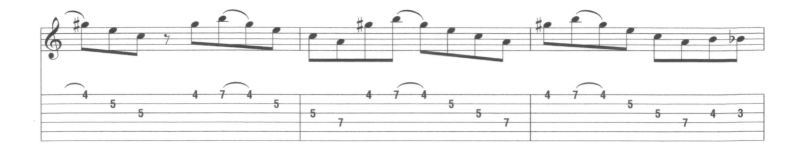

Am7

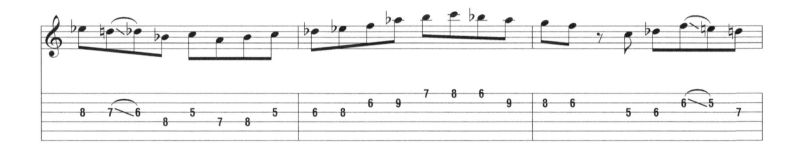

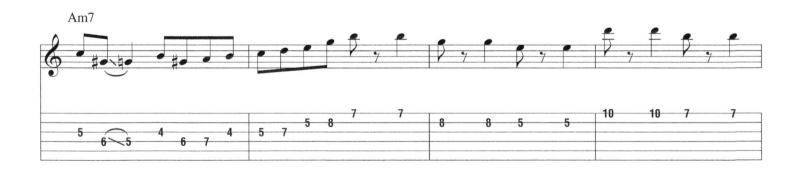

*Gtr. and bass exchange 4 meas. solos
("trade fours") throughout section.

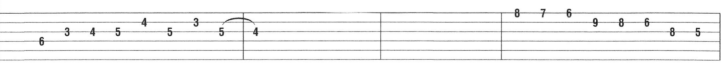

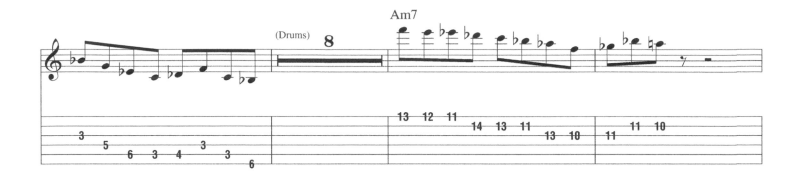

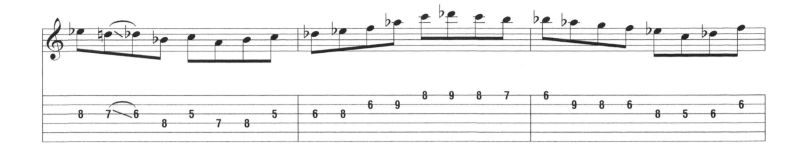

D.S. al Coda

(Drums) **8**

Coda

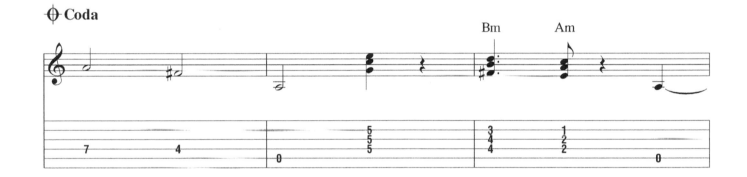

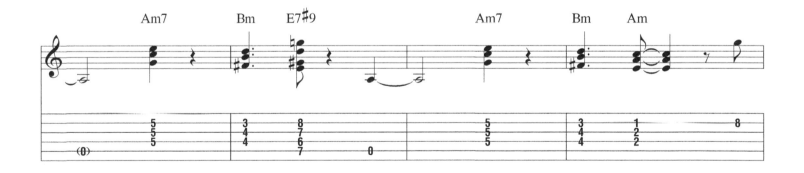

Free time

Moonlight in Vermont

Words and Music by John Blackburn and Karl Suessdorf

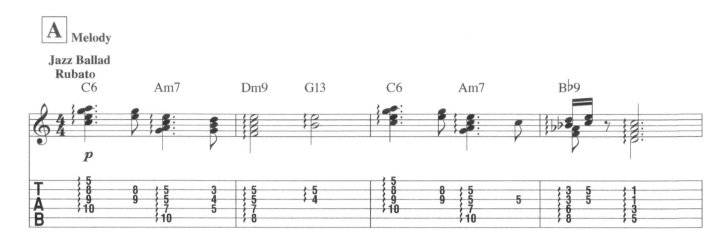

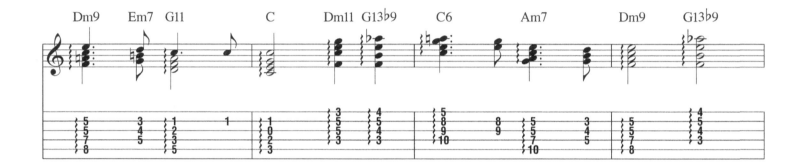

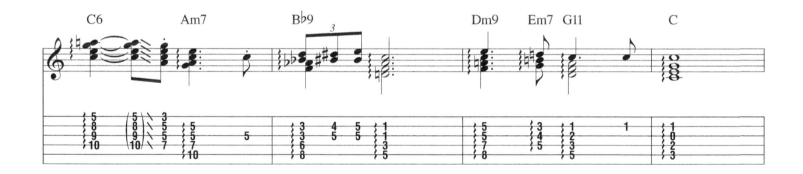

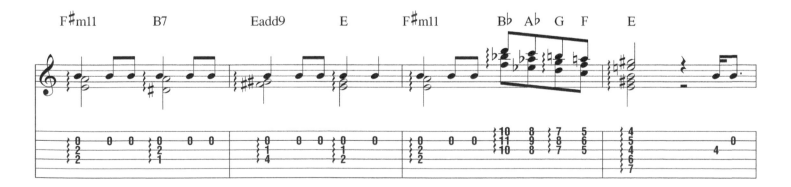

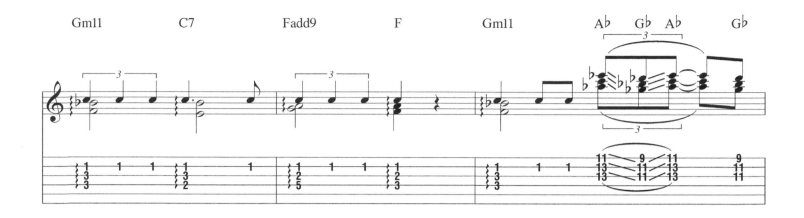

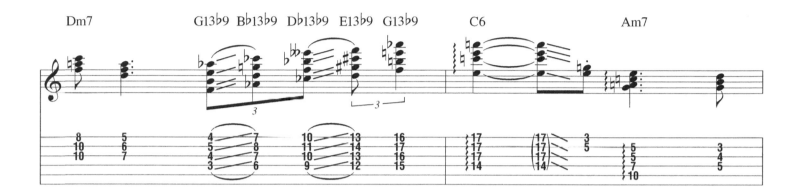

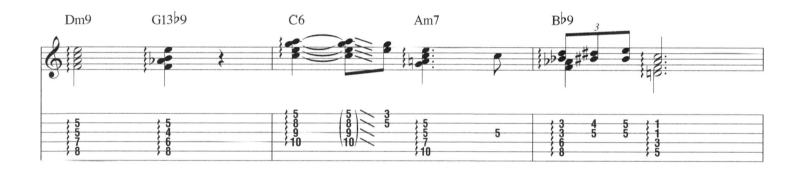

B Alto Sax Solo

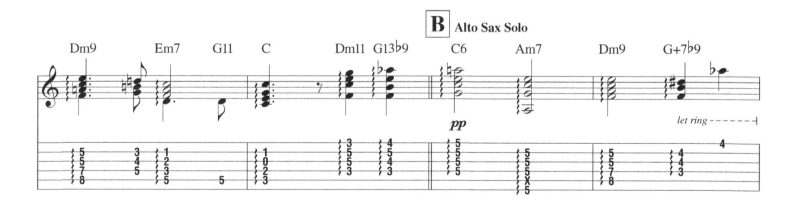

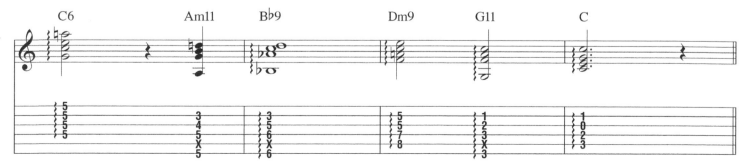

C Guitar Solo

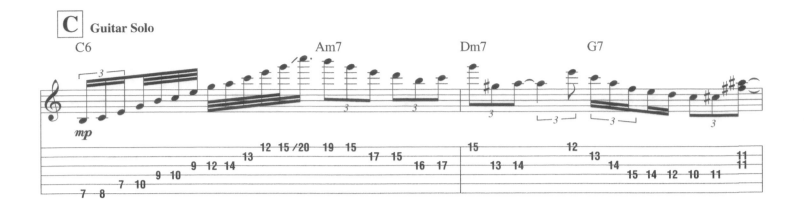

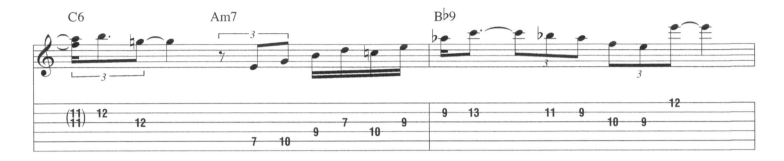

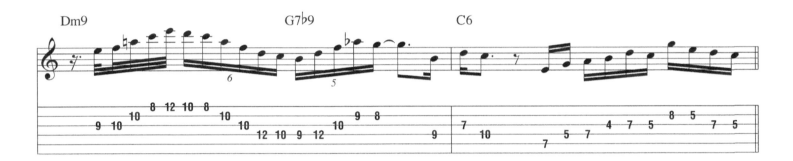

D Bass Solo

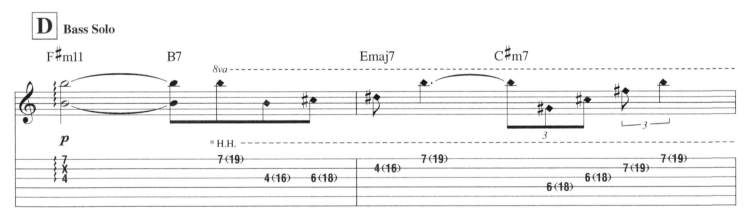

*Fret the note normally, and produce a harmonic by gently resting the pick hand's index finger directly above the indicated fret (in parentheses) while the pick hand's thumb or pick assists by plucking the appropriate string.

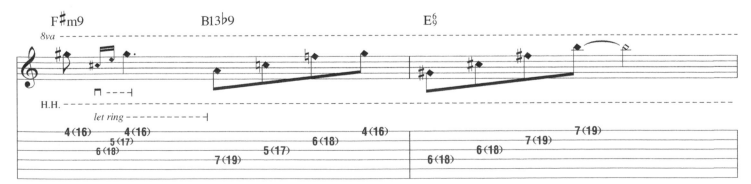

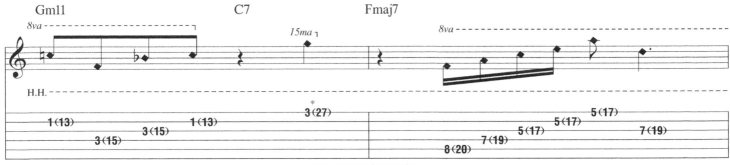

*Hypothetical fret location.

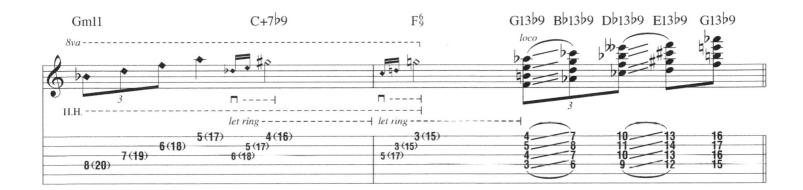

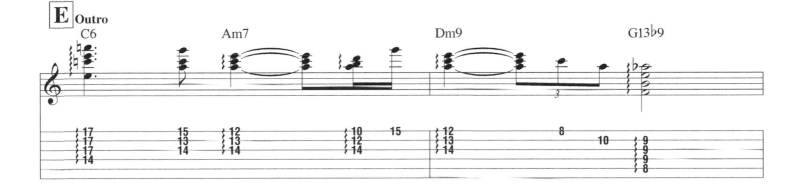

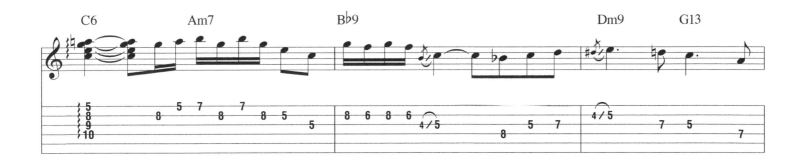

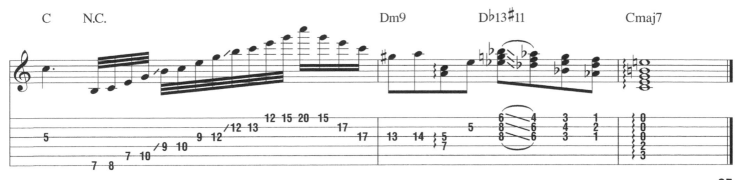

On a Slow Boat to China

By Frank Loesser

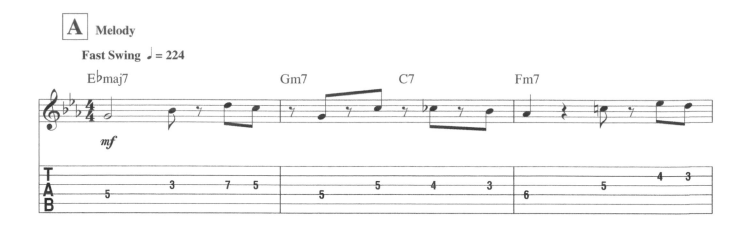

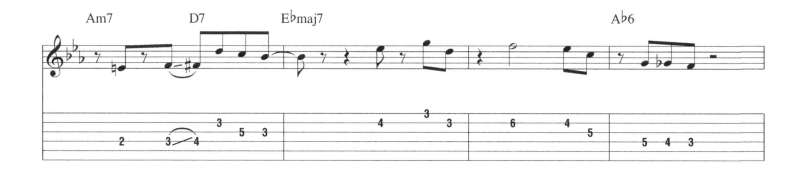

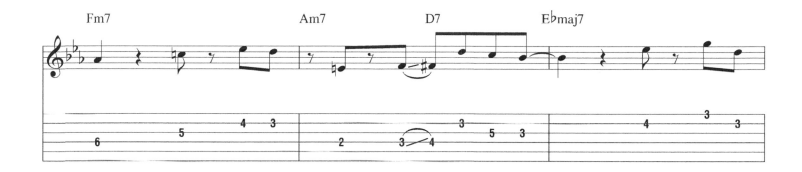

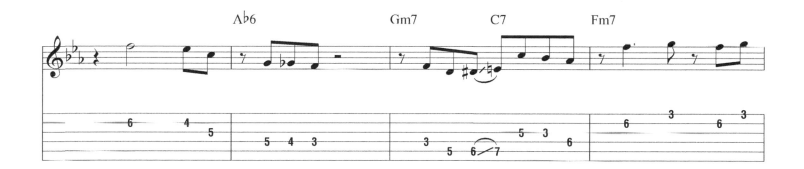

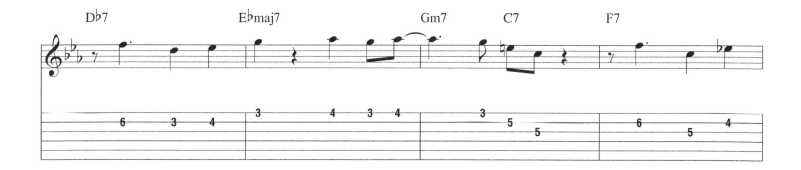

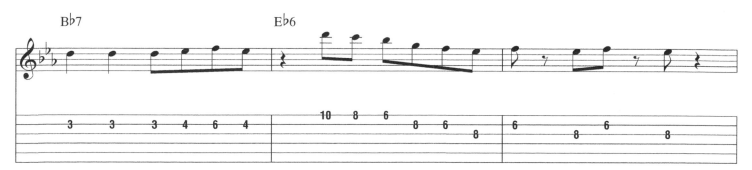

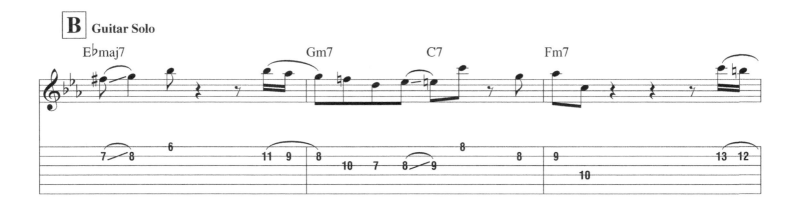

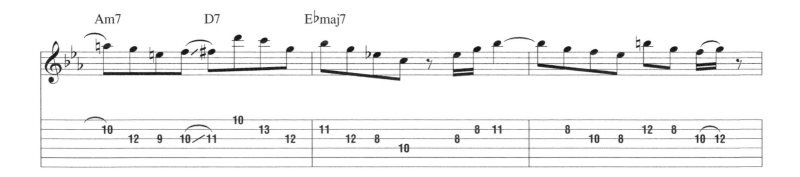

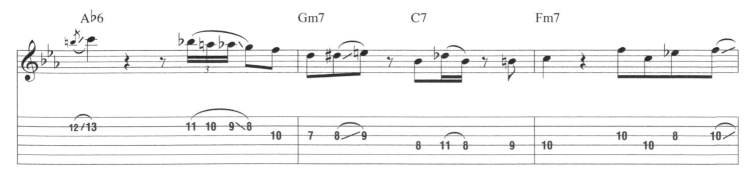

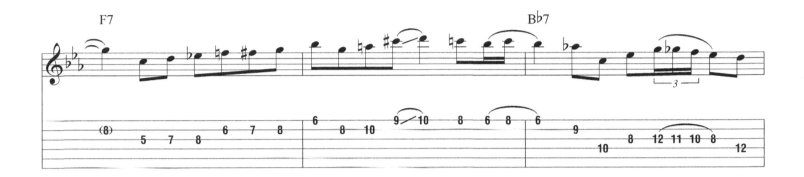

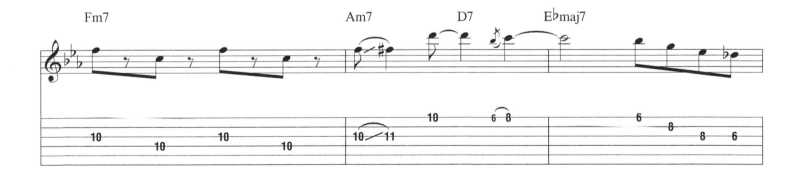

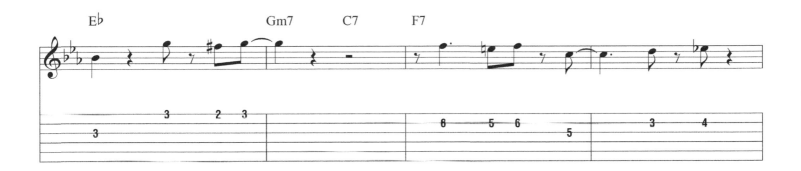

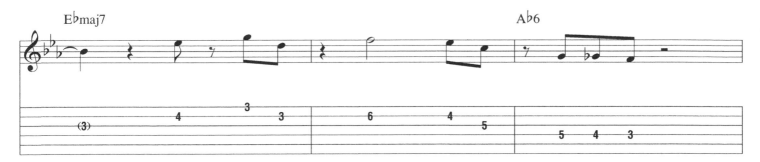

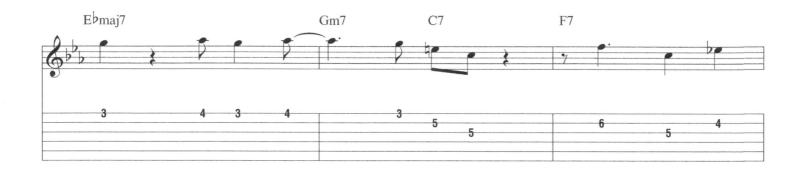

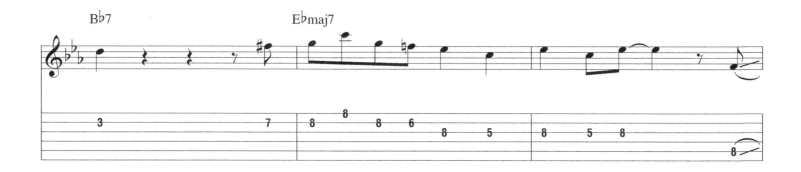

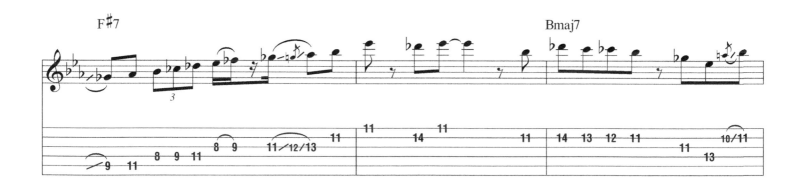

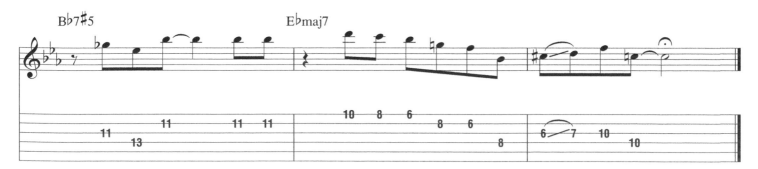

Things Ain't What They Used to Be

By Mercer Ellington

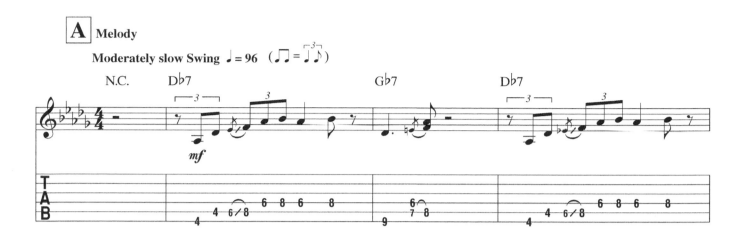

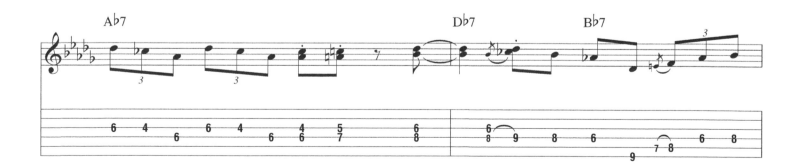

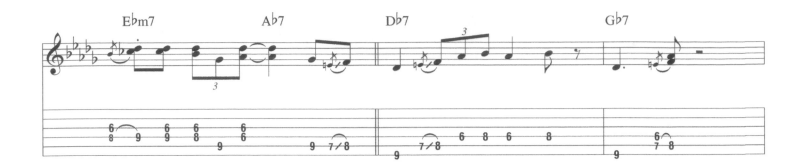

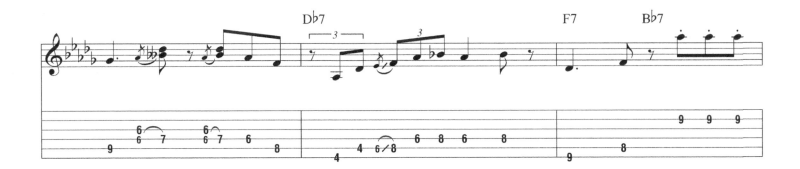

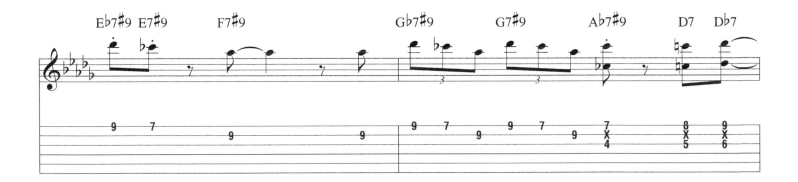

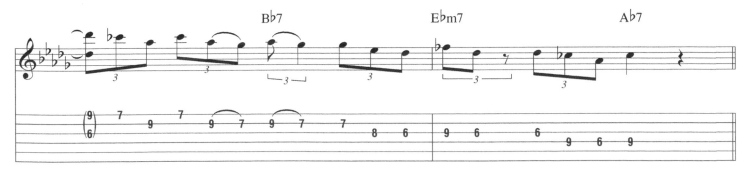

Guitar Solo

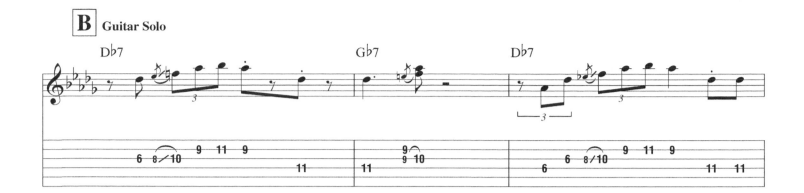

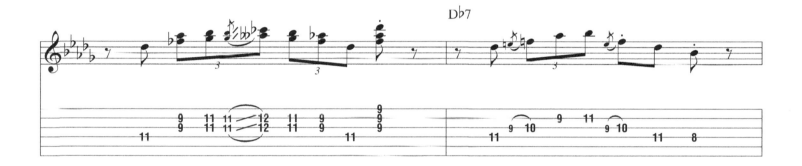

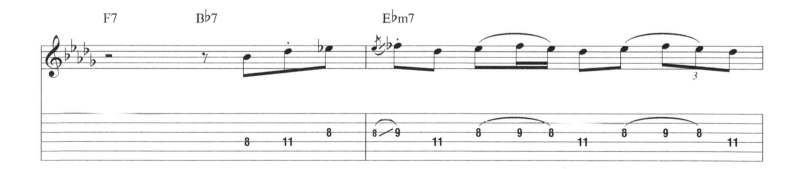

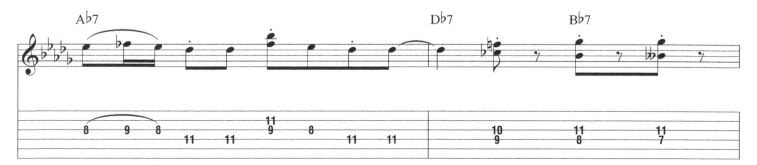

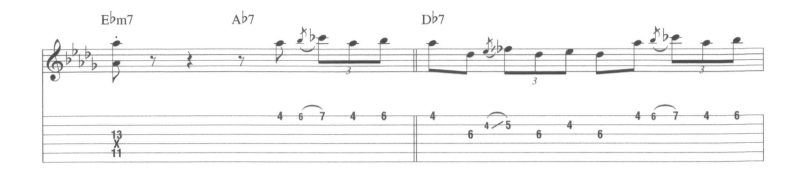

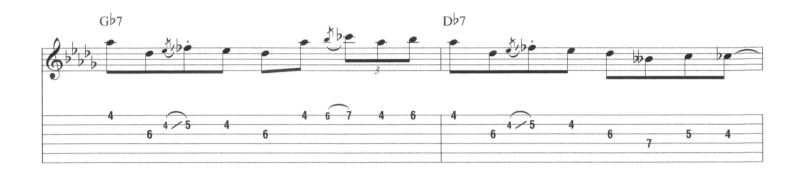

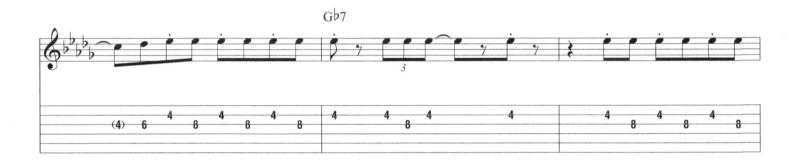

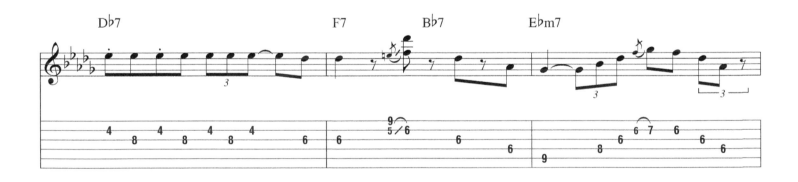

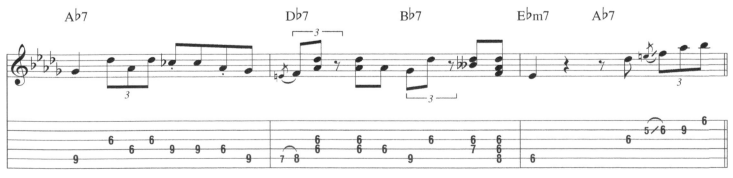

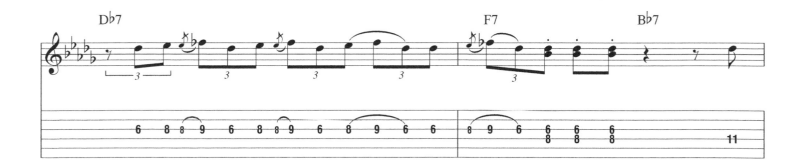

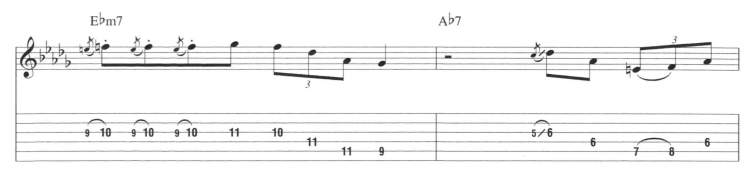

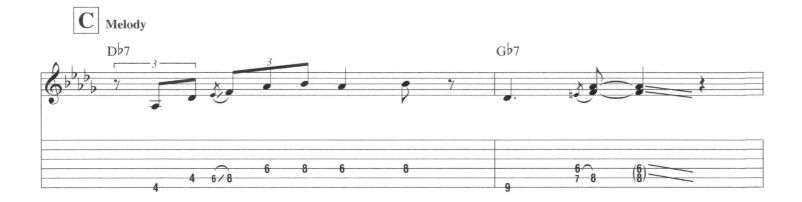

C Melody

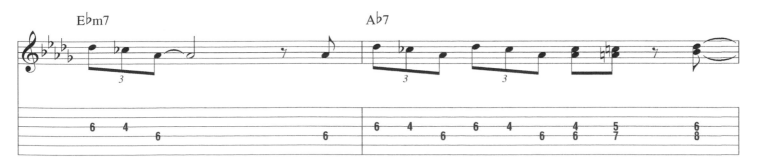

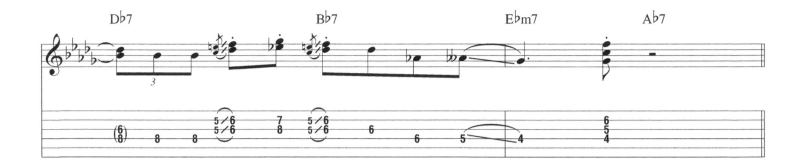

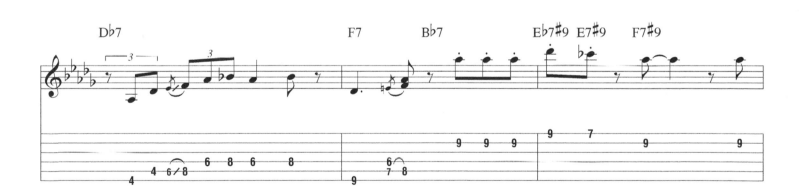

Yesterdays

Words by Otto Harbach
Music by Jerome Kern

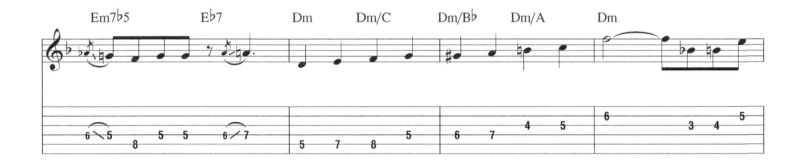

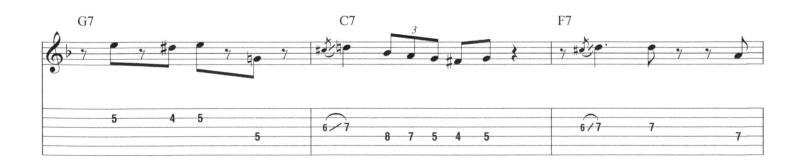

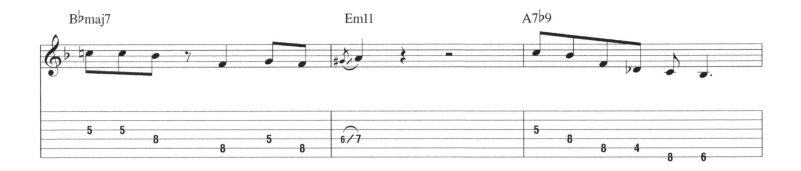

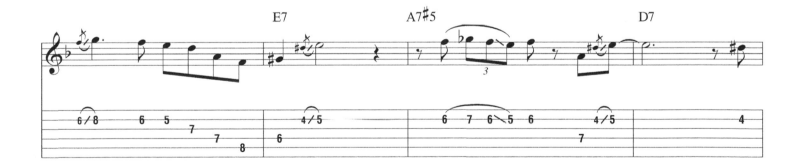

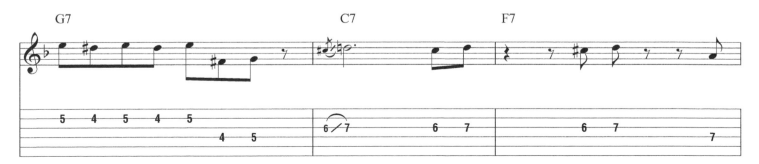

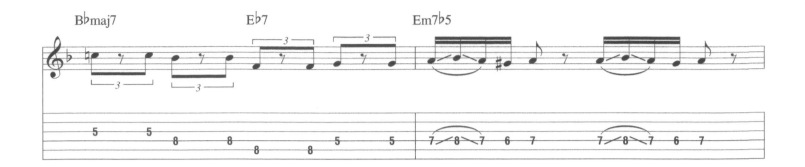

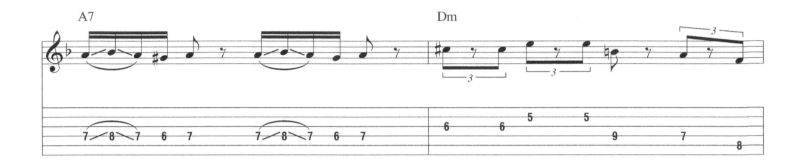

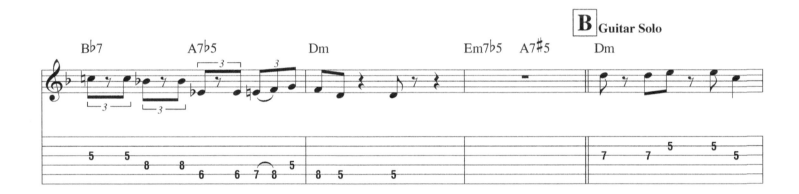

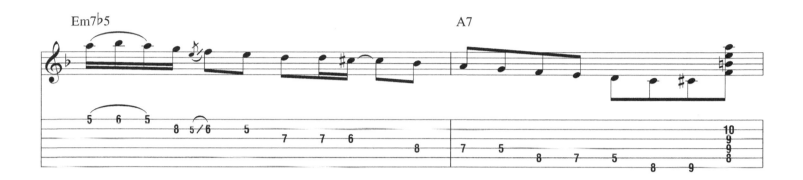

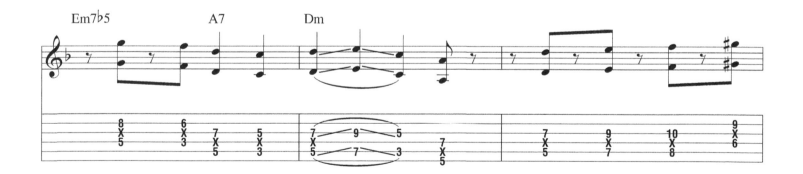

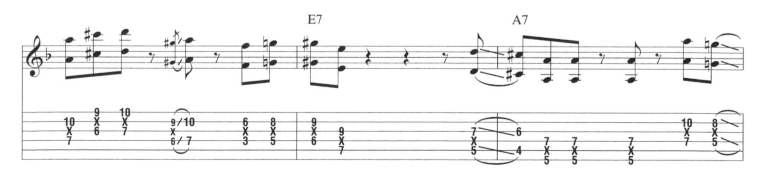

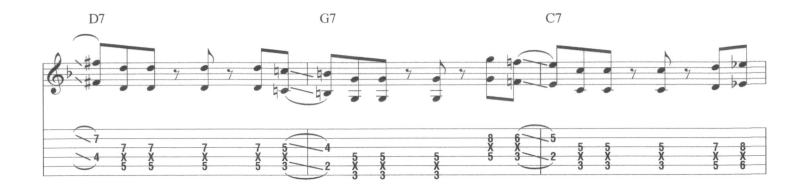

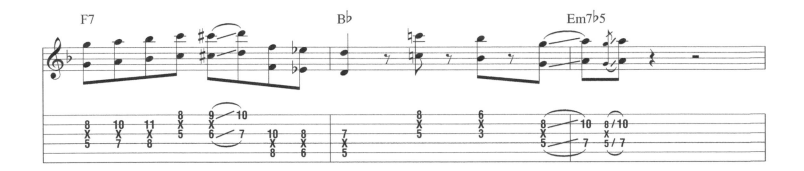

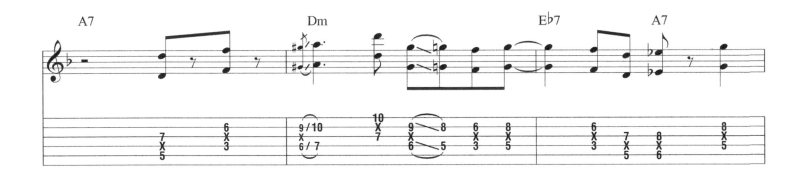

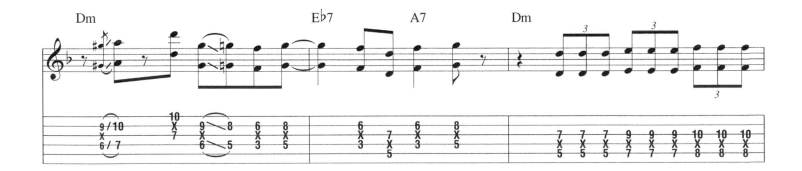

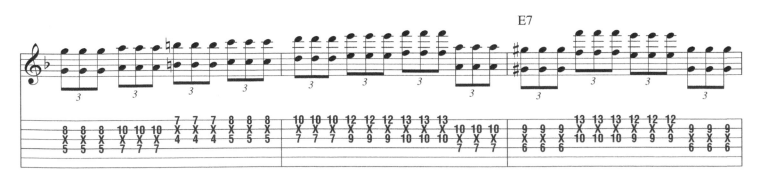

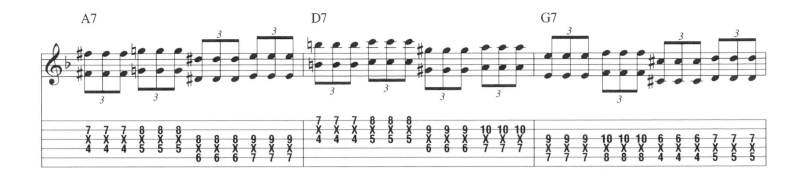

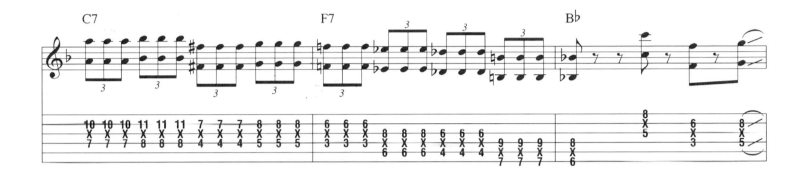

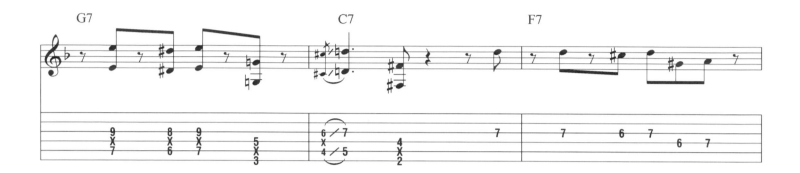

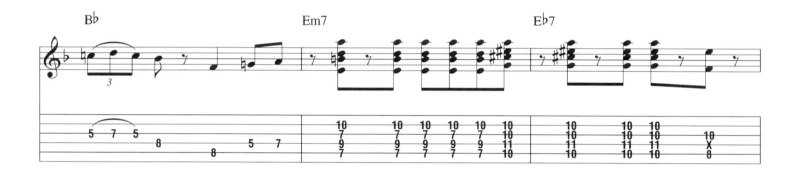

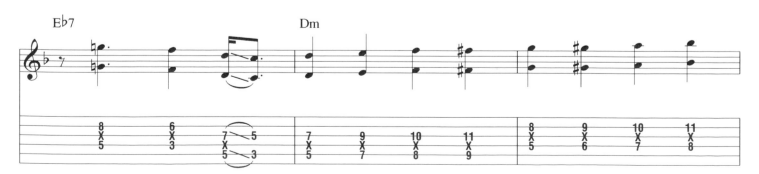

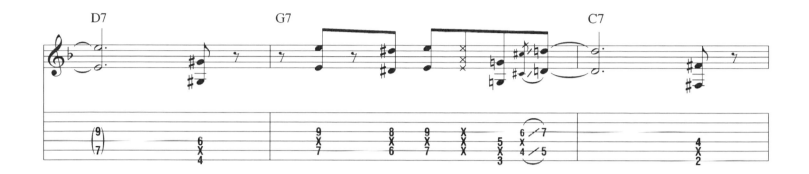

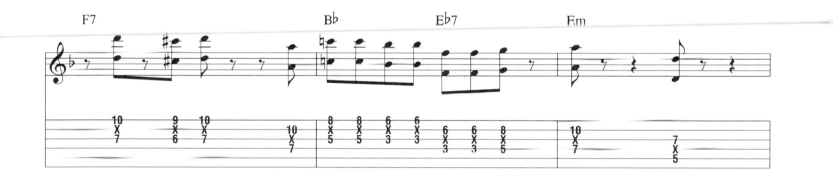

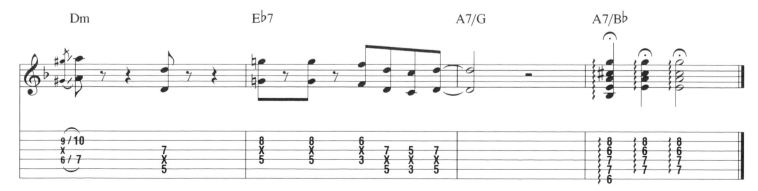

HAL•LEONARD' GUITAR PLAY-ALONG

Complete song lists available online.

This series will help you play your favorite songs quickly and easily. Just follow the tab and listen to the audio to the hear how the guitar should sound, and then play along using the separate backing tracks. Audio files also include software to slow down the tempo without changing pitch. The melody and lyrics are included in the book so that you can sing or simply follow along.

INCLUDES TAB

VOL. 1 – ROCK	00699570 / $17.99	
VOL. 2 – ACOUSTIC	00699569 / $16.99	
VOL. 3 – HARD ROCK	00699573 / $17.99	
VOL. 4 – POP/ROCK	00699571 / $16.99	
VOL. 5 – THREE CHORD SONGS	00300985 / $16.99	
VOL. 6 – '90S ROCK	00298615 / $16.99	
VOL. 7 – BLUES	00699575 / $19.99	
VOL. 8 – ROCK	00699585 / $16.99	
VOL. 9 – EASY ACOUSTIC SONGS	00151708 / $16.99	
VOL. 10 – ACOUSTIC	00699586 / $16.95	
VOL. 11 – EARLY ROCK	00699579 / $15.99	
VOL. 12 – ROCK POP	00291724 / $16.99	
VOL. 14 – BLUES ROCK	00699582 / $16.99	
VOL. 15 – R&B	00699583 / $17.99	
VOL. 16 – JAZZ	00699584 / $16.99	
VOL. 17 – COUNTRY	00699588 / $17.99	
VOL. 18 – ACOUSTIC ROCK	00699577 / $15.95	
VOL. 20 – ROCKABILLY	00699580 / $17.99	
VOL. 21 – SANTANA	00174525 / $17.99	
VOL. 22 – CHRISTMAS	00699600 / $15.99	
VOL. 23 – SURF	00699635 / $17.99	
VOL. 24 – ERIC CLAPTON	00699649 / $19.99	
VOL. 25 – THE BEATLES	00198265 / $19.99	
VOL. 26 – ELVIS PRESLEY	00699643 / $16.99	
VOL. 27 – DAVID LEE ROTH	00699645 / $16.95	
VOL. 28 – GREG KOCH	00699646 / $19.99	
VOL. 29 – BOB SEGER	00699647 / $16.99	
VOL. 30 – KISS	00699644 / $17.99	
VOL. 32 – THE OFFSPRING	00699653 / $14.95	
VOL. 33 – ACOUSTIC CLASSICS	00699656 / $19.99	
VOL. 34 – CLASSIC ROCK	00699658 / $17.99	
VOL. 35 – HAIR METAL	00699660 / $17.99	
VOL. 36 – SOUTHERN ROCK	00699661 / $19.99	
VOL. 37 – ACOUSTIC UNPLUGGED	00699662 / $22.99	
VOL. 38 – BLUES	00699663 / $17.99	
VOL. 39 – '80s METAL	00699664 / $17.99	
VOL. 40 – INCUBUS	00699668 / $17.95	
VOL. 41 – ERIC CLAPTON	00699669 / $17.99	
VOL. 42 – COVER BAND HITS	00211597 / $16.99	
VOL. 43 – LYNYRD SKYNYRD	00699681 / $22.99	
VOL. 44 – JAZZ GREATS	00699689 / $16.99	
VOL. 45 – TV THEMES	00699718 / $14.95	
VOL. 46 – MAINSTREAM ROCK	00699722 / $16.95	
VOL. 47 – JIMI HENDRIX SMASH HITS	00699723 / $19.99	
VOL. 48 – AEROSMITH CLASSICS	00699724 / $17.99	
VOL. 49 – STEVIE RAY VAUGHAN	00699725 / $17.99	
VOL. 50 – VAN HALEN: 1978-1984	00110269 / $19.99	
VOL. 51 – ALTERNATIVE '90s	00699727 / $14.99	
VOL. 52 – FUNK	00699728 / $15.99	
VOL. 53 – DISCO	00699729 / $14.99	
VOL. 54 – HEAVY METAL	00699730 / $17.99	
VOL. 55 – POP METAL	00699731 / $14.95	
VOL. 57 – GUNS 'N' ROSES	00159922 / $19.99	
VOL. 58 – BLINK 182	00699772 / $17.99	
VOL. 59 – CHET ATKINS	00702347 / $17.99	
VOL. 60 – 3 DOORS DOWN	00699774 / $14.95	
VOL. 62 – CHRISTMAS CAROLS	00699798 / $12.95	
VOL. 63 – CREEDENCE CLEARWATER REVIVAL	00699802 / $17.99	
VOL. 64 – ULTIMATE OZZY OSBOURNE	00699803 / $19.99	
VOL. 66 – THE ROLLING STONES	00699807 / $19.99	
VOL. 67 – BLACK SABBATH	00699808 / $17.99	
VOL. 68 – PINK FLOYD – DARK SIDE OF THE MOON	00699809 / $17.99	
VOL. 71 – CHRISTIAN ROCK	00699824 / $14.95	
VOL. 73 – BLUESY ROCK	00699829 / $17.99	
VOL. 74 – SIMPLE STRUMMING SONGS	00151706 / $19.99	
VOL. 75 – TOM PETTY	00699882 / $19.99	
VOL. 76 – COUNTRY HITS	00699884 / $16.99	
VOL. 77 – BLUEGRASS	00699910 / $17.99	
VOL. 78 – NIRVANA	00700132 / $17.99	
VOL. 79 – NEIL YOUNG	00700133 / $24.99	
VOL. 81 – ROCK ANTHOLOGY	00700176 / $22.99	
VOL. 82 – EASY ROCK SONGS	00700177 / $17.99	
VOL. 84 – STEELY DAN	00700200 / $19.99	
VOL. 85 – THE POLICE	00700269 / $16.99	
VOL. 86 – BOSTON	00700465 / $19.99	
VOL. 87 – ACOUSTIC WOMEN	00700763 / $14.99	
VOL. 88 – GRUNGE	00700467 / $16.99	
VOL. 89 – REGGAE	00700468 / $15.99	
VOL. 90 – CLASSICAL POP	00700469 / $14.99	
VOL. 91 – BLUES INSTRUMENTALS	00700505 / $19.99	
VOL. 92 – EARLY ROCK INSTRUMENTALS	00700506 / $17.99	
VOL. 93 – ROCK INSTRUMENTALS	00700507 / $17.99	
VOL. 94 – SLOW BLUES	00700508 / $16.99	
VOL. 95 – BLUES CLASSICS	00700509 / $15.99	
VOL. 96 – BEST COUNTRY HITS	00211615 / $16.99	
VOL. 97 – CHRISTMAS CLASSICS	00236542 / $14.99	
VOL. 99 – ZZ TOP	00700762 / $16.99	
VOL. 100 – B.B. KING	00700466 / $16.99	
VOL. 101 – SONGS FOR BEGINNERS	00701917 / $14.99	
VOL. 102 – CLASSIC PUNK	00700769 / $14.99	
VOL. 104 – DUANE ALLMAN	00700846 / $22.99	
VOL. 105 – LATIN	00700939 / $16.99	
VOL. 106 – WEEZER	00700958 / $17.99	
VOL. 107 – CREAM	00701069 / $17.99	
VOL. 108 – THE WHO	00701053 / $17.99	
VOL. 109 – STEVE MILLER	00701054 / $19.99	
VOL. 110 – SLIDE GUITAR HITS	00701055 / $17.99	
VOL. 111 – JOHN MELLENCAMP	00701056 / $14.99	
VOL. 112 – QUEEN	00701052 / $16.99	
VOL. 113 – JIM CROCE	00701058 / $19.99	
VOL. 114 – BON JOVI	00701060 / $17.99	
VOL. 115 – JOHNNY CASH	00701070 / $17.99	
VOL. 116 – THE VENTURES	00701124 / $17.99	
VOL. 117 – BRAD PAISLEY	00701224 / $16.99	
VOL. 118 – ERIC JOHNSON	00701353 / $17.99	
VOL. 119 – AC/DC CLASSICS	00701356 / $19.99	
VOL. 120 – PROGRESSIVE ROCK	00701457 / $14.99	
VOL. 121 – U2	00701508 / $17.99	
VOL. 122 – CROSBY, STILLS & NASH	00701610 / $16.99	
VOL. 123 – LENNON & McCARTNEY ACOUSTIC	00701614 / $16.99	
VOL. 124 – SMOOTH JAZZ	00200664 / $16.99	
VOL. 125 – JEFF BECK	00701687 / $19.99	
VOL. 126 – BOB MARLEY	00701701 / $17.99	
VOL. 127 – 1970s ROCK	00701739 / $17.99	
VOL. 128 – 1960s ROCK	00701740 / $14.99	
VOL. 129 – MEGADETH	00701741 / $17.99	
VOL. 130 – IRON MAIDEN	00701742 / $17.99	
VOL. 131 – 1990s ROCK	00701743 / $14.99	
VOL. 132 – COUNTRY ROCK	00701757 / $15.99	
VOL. 133 – TAYLOR SWIFT	00701894 / $16.99	
VOL. 135 – MINOR BLUES	00151350 / $17.99	
VOL. 136 – GUITAR THEMES	00701922 / $14.99	
VOL. 137 – IRISH TUNES	00701966 / $15.99	
VOL. 138 – BLUEGRASS CLASSICS	00701967 / $17.99	
VOL. 139 – GARY MOORE	00702370 / $17.99	
VOL. 140 – MORE STEVIE RAY VAUGHAN	00702396 / $19.99	
VOL. 141 – ACOUSTIC HITS	00702401 / $16.99	
VOL. 142 – GEORGE HARRISON	00237697 / $17.99	
VOL. 143 – SLASH	00702425 / $19.99	
VOL. 144 – DJANGO REINHARDT	00702531 / $17.99	
VOL. 145 – DEF LEPPARD	00702532 / $19.99	
VOL. 146 – ROBERT JOHNSON	00702533 / $16.99	
VOL. 147 – SIMON & GARFUNKEL	14041591 / $17.99	
VOL. 148 – BOB DYLAN	14041592 / $17.99	
VOL. 149 – AC/DC HITS	14041593 / $19.99	
VOL. 150 – ZAKK WYLDE	02501717 / $19.99	
VOL. 151 – J.S. BACH	02501730 / $16.99	
VOL. 152 – JOE BONAMASSA	02501751 / $24.99	
VOL. 153 – RED HOT CHILI PEPPERS	00702990 / $22.99	
VOL. 155 – ERIC CLAPTON UNPLUGGED	00703085 / $17.99	
VOL. 156 – SLAYER	00703770 / $19.99	
VOL. 157 – FLEETWOOD MAC	00101382 / $17.99	
VOL. 159 – WES MONTGOMERY	00102593 / $22.99	
VOL. 160 – T-BONE WALKER	00102641 / $17.99	
VOL. 161 – THE EAGLES ACOUSTIC	00102659 / $19.99	
VOL. 162 – THE EAGLES HITS	00102667 / $17.99	
VOL. 163 – PANTERA	00103036 / $19.99	
VOL. 164 – VAN HALEN: 1986-1995	00110270 / $19.99	
VOL. 165 – GREEN DAY	00210343 / $17.99	
VOL. 166 – MODERN BLUES	00700764 / $16.99	
VOL. 167 – DREAM THEATER	00111938 / $24.99	
VOL. 168 – KISS	00113421 / $17.99	
VOL. 169 – TAYLOR SWIFT	00115982 / $16.99	
VOL. 170 – THREE DAYS GRACE	00117337 / $16.99	
VOL. 171 – JAMES BROWN	00117420 / $16.99	
VOL. 172 – THE DOOBIE BROTHERS	00119670 / $17.99	
VOL. 173 – TRANS-SIBERIAN ORCHESTRA	00119907 / $19.99	
VOL. 174 – SCORPIONS	00122119 / $19.99	
VOL. 175 – MICHAEL SCHENKER	00122127 / $17.99	
VOL. 176 – BLUES BREAKERS WITH JOHN MAYALL & ERIC CLAPTON	00122132 / $19.99	
VOL. 177 – ALBERT KING	00123271 / $17.99	
VOL. 178 – JASON MRAZ	00124165 / $17.99	
VOL. 179 – RAMONES	00127073 / $16.99	
VOL. 180 – BRUNO MARS	00129706 / $16.99	
VOL. 181 – JACK JOHNSON	00129854 / $16.99	
VOL. 182 – SOUNDGARDEN	00138161 / $17.99	
VOL. 183 – BUDDY GUY	00138240 / $17.99	
VOL. 184 – KENNY WAYNE SHEPHERD	00138258 / $17.99	
VOL. 185 – JOE SATRIANI	00139457 / $19.99	
VOL. 186 – GRATEFUL DEAD	00139459 / $17.99	
VOL. 187 – JOHN DENVER	00140839 / $19.99	
VOL. 188 – MÖTLEY CRÜE	00141145 / $19.99	
VOL. 189 – JOHN MAYER	00144350 / $19.99	
VOL. 190 – DEEP PURPLE	00146152 / $19.99	
VOL. 191 – PINK FLOYD CLASSICS	00146164 / $17.99	
VOL. 192 – JUDAS PRIEST	00151352 / $19.99	
VOL. 193 – STEVE VAI	00156028 / $19.99	
VOL. 194 – PEARL JAM	00157925 / $17.99	
VOL. 195 – METALLICA: 1983-1988	00234291 / $22.99	
VOL. 196 – METALLICA: 1991-2016	00234292 / $19.99	

Prices, contents, and availability subject to change without notice.

HAL•LEONARD®

www.halleonard.com